Case Against the Science of Climate Change

(Pamphlet)

Michael A. Ioffe B.Sc

In memory of Tatyana Ioffe (01/22/1949-01/10/2012)

Contents

Introduction

It is impossible to read all the books, articles, and other sources about climate-driven theories, suggestions, and aspects about nature. Of course, sun energy is the main engine in the Earth's climate, but I read articles about this topic and think that it is better to choose points of the scientists who blame carbon dioxide for the recent climate change. I believe these points deserve a closer look, more so than any other theories.

Why do I think so?

It is because of their point to blame mankind's activities in the changing of climate. If mankind's activities could influence climate, it provides hope that mankind could influence climate right now. Instead of looking at the Sun's position to the Earth from more than 100,000 years ago and pray to Ra as the ancient Egyptians did, our civilization is mature enough to prepare for any predictable changes in the near future. It could create hope about human influence on the climate; of course with some limits during any changes in sun energy received by the Earth during very warm, as right now or even cold as in the glacier period.

At the same time, I think that today's science of climate change is making a huge mistake by blaming greenhouse gases (GHG) for climate change. In my opinion, GHG are only indicators of human activities and we have other reasons for climate change. Thinking about these possibilities, I hope that I have found engineering solutions to fight climate change with the help of only three countries in the world—USA, Canada, and Mexico. I am sure that we could do it with the huge profits from these countries. Their effort could provide the populations of these countries job security for at least the next twenty to fifty years, despite the globalization in the world today. We don't need to blame globalization anymore and must enjoy its cheap prices for most products, which we need. I am not an economist, but looking at how the Bush and Obama administrations so badly tried and failed with their attempts to revolt the economy, I begin to think that economists from both parties were/are living somewhere in the1980s when Jack Welch, CEO of GE, and his followers opened businesses in China and other developmental countries. For good or bad, they spent more than thirty years to bring us to today's crisis with employment and the economy. If somebody wants to spend another thirty years to go back, I want to remind them about what happened in the former Russian Empire after 1917.

The former Soviet Union badly tried to create a new "socialist economy" but never reached the prosperity of the US and Western European countries. Stalin, Khrushchev, Brezhnev, and Gorbachev all promised the Soviet people a dream to live in prosperity from communism and failed. Ideas to build a new economy by crushing the old one never work.

Boris Yeltsin vowed to transform Russia's socialist command economy in to a free <u>market economy</u>, implement economic shock therapy, price liberalization, and privatize programs. Due to the method of privatization, a good deal of the national wealth fell into the hands of a small group of oligarchs. That was in 1990s and until now, the economy of Russia was not so great for a country as rich in resources as Russia. The government of China took lessons from Russia, and their own turmoil, and made better choices to improve their economy. We do not need to intervene in this process and return to the 1980s. It will be not good for the US, China, Russia, or the rest of the world. We must use any achievements in our and the world economy and never go back. We must find new directions in the new globalization environment. I will try to show to readers these directions, which I found studying the science of climate change.

In my opinion, scientists of climate change did—and are doing right now—a huge job, and mostly not in science, but in political propaganda of their ideas. Their science is wrong, but they are so sure that they are right that every newspaper and magazine is publishing articles mentioning climate change almost every day. The United Nations, governments around the world, writers, scientists, movies, they are full of predictions about the extinction of animals and vegetation; about oceans rising, hunger in the world, floods, droughts, hurricanes, and many other disasters which will face mankind in near future. Reading them, I always have mixed feelings how they correct in descriptions of all these disasters, and how they are wrong in reasons. We need to ask questions like, "Why it will happen? What are the real reasons for climate change? What must we do to prevent or prepare for these changes?"

As a physicist by education and a design engineer by experience, after retirement in 2004, I quickly caught on to the main problems with the science of climate change. It was a long way for me to try to bring attention to this problem to the public. This book is a new attempt for me to change the minds of billions of people about these problems in the world. Despite the use of some math calculations—all of them are on the level of math in middle school—I am sure that every person can easily understand and double check my calculations. I think that everyone who agrees or disagrees with the science of climate change can find something new in this book.

Science is not a dogma; scientists are not smarter than you are. Please do not be afraid to question any scientist's position. Scientists, of course, are more informed than anyone of us is about a specific subject, but when they are writing about their ideas, we could check these ideas with our previous knowledge. We have advantages in taking a fresh look at their points. And even if they are right, our skeptical view will only help us to better understand their ideas. Please, be skeptical of everything that you are reading, including this book. Please, do not be afraid to be skeptical of not only new knowledge, but also even of what you think you know very well. If you are reading about the same subject again and again, you are missing some nuances because you made decisions in your mind about the topic long ago. I invite you to forget about what you read or heard about climate change and reevaluate your knowledge as if you were hearing about it for the first time.

Preface

Weather Extremes Hint At Climate Change Health Impact...

A corn crop dries in a field on July 28, 2011 near Perryton, Texas...

Drought in Zimbabwe...

Articles like these are in every newspaper, magazine, and on every news channel every day to keep people in a panic mood. Are these scientific facts or a simple propaganda machine working to make a connection with billions of frightened people to fight for something against the most unclear phenomenon in nature? Or is it a huge mistake on an Aristotle level, that the Earth is the center of the universe? Is it new or was it long before?

Let's look at some history.

Nikita Khrushchev organized The Virgin Lands Campaign in the northern Kazakhstan and the Altay regions of Russia. There was 190,000 km^2 in tilled land in 1954 and an extra 140,000 km^2 in 1955. More than 300,000 people arrived in the Virgin Lands to begin new lives as farmers. Hundreds of thousands of soldiers, students, and combine harvester operators joined them to help harvest. The first harvest in 1956 was a stunning success. The Soviet Union produced, per capita, twice as much wheat as the West. By the 1960s, the soil had been drained of all its nutrients beneficial to wheat. Nobody even tried to prevent erosion and very soon, soil was simply being blown away by the wind, leaving bare, useless steppe behind.

The Aral Sea was a lake that lay between Kazakhstan in the north and Karakalpakstan, an autonomous region of Uzbekistan, in the south. It was one of the four largest lakes in the world with an area of 68,000 square kilometers. The Aral Sea had been steadily shrinking since the 1960s after the rivers that fed it were diverted by Soviet Union irrigation projects. By 2007, it had declined to 10% of its original size.

Let look at article: *12 Aug 2011 "Drought-hit Zimbabwe farmers push Government to lift GMO ban. Trust.org/alertnet.*

> *Volatile climatic patterns in southern Zimbabwe's Matebeleland, particularly in low-rainfall rural areas like Gwanda, south of Bulawayo, are seeing farmer livelihoods being destroyed with little they can do to mitigate their losses."*

Farmers are trying to use genetically modified organisms (GMOs), in this case corn, to reduce the influence of drought. What was missed in this article is that between 1990 and 2005, Zimbabwe lost 21% of its forest cover to fields of corn. It was done for area, which has a history of drought. This history we could find in next article:

> *1994 Zimbabwe: Landuse in Dry Tropical SavannasState of the environment in Southern Africa, SADC*

> *An historical overview of drought and rainfall patterns in Southern Africa since 1800 is given below: 1820–30 This was a decade of severe drought throughout Africa.*

> *1844–49 Southern Africa experienced five consecutive drought years.*

> *1870–90 This period was humid in some areas and former Lake Ngami, in the northwest of Botswana, was full.*

> *1875–1910 There was a marked decrease in rainfall in southern Africa, and 1910 experienced a severe drought.*

> *1921–30 Severe droughts in the region.*

> *1930–50 Southern Africa experienced dry periods alternating with wet ones, and in some years, the rains were very good. The 1946–47 seasons experienced a severe drought.*

> *1950s There was abnormally high rainfall in some parts of the region. East Africa experienced flooding, and Lake Victoria rose by*

several meters. Elsewhere, the equatorial region experienced below normal rainfall.

1967–73 This six-year period was dry across the southern African region. The equatorial region experienced above average rainfall.

1974–80 This period of six years was relatively moist over much of southern Africa. In 1974, the average annual rainfall was 100 percent above normal throughout the region. 1981–82 Most of southern Africa experienced drought.

1982 Most of sub-tropical Africa experienced drought.

1983 This was a particularly bad drought year for the entire African continent.

1985 Conditions improved.

1986–87 Drought conditions returned.

1991–92 Southern Africa, excluding Namibia, experienced the worst drought in living memory.

What are the reasons for the increasing of "the worst drought in living memory"in Africa, the erosion of land on the Virgin Lands of Kazakhstan, and the shrinking of the Aral Sea?Is it due to the increase of carbon dioxide and other GHG emitted by machinery to till the land, irrigate cotton fields, and cut forests for corn production? And if so, why exactly are these areas more damaged by human activities? Do we have "special GHG" in all those areas, which "forget" how to distribute themselves around the world?

A corn crop dries in a field on July 28, 2011 near Perriton, Texas...

Drought in Zimbabwe...

Erosion of Virgin Land...

Shrinking of the Aral Sea...

All of these statements are the result of human activities, the same as in many other places in all continents with arable land. All of these activities, of course, increase the amount of greenhouse gases (GHG) in the atmosphere. At the same time, it is impossible for nature to be so precise in response. It is the main argument against GHG theory in climate change.

Ghg Are Not Guilty!

GHG are only indicator of human activities, because we use mostly fossil sources of energy for our needs. Human activities changed continents, and these changes are real reasons for climate change. These changes are proportional to increase of amount of GHG in atmosphere. It is easy to calculate changes in the atmosphere of carbon dioxide and other GHG by human activities. If scientists believe that these changes are responsible for climate change, it is easy to put the coefficient of the changes into computer models; and computers will show exactly that the result of global warming is proportional to the increasing amount of GHG in the atmosphere. If climate change really is because of changes on continents by human activities, we are making the wrong suggestions on how to save the world. In this case, all recommendations from scientists are dead wrong.

Let's make an evaluation of two different points of view.

Today, the science of climate change is claiming the following:

Mankind's activities increase the amount of carbon dioxide in the air. Carbon dioxide is GHG and because of that, the temperature is increased. In hot air, there will be more water vapor, which is also GHG, and because of that, the temperature will increase more. Water vapor is playing positive feedback in climate change.

In opposition to the opinion of most scientists of climate change, however, claims the following:

Properties of water are actually cooling the atmosphere, despite water vapor being GHG.

IT IS VERY IMPORTANT FOR OUR ECONOMY AND FOR OUR FUTURE ON A WORLDWIDE SCALE TO CHOOSE A SIDE.

The following comes from a 2007 report by The Associated Press in Bangkok, Thailand: *"Cities around the world are facing the danger of rising seas and other disasters related to climate change.*

Of the 33 cities predicted to have at least 8 million people by 2015, at least 21 are highly vulnerable, says the Worldwatch Institute.

They include Dhaka, Bangladesh; Buenos Aires, Argentina; Rio de Janeiro, Brazil; Shanghai and Tianjin in China; Alexandria and Cairo in Egypt; Mumbai and Kolkata in India; Jakarta, Indonesia; Tokyo and Osaka-Kobe in Japan; Lagos, Nigeria; Karachi, Pakistan; Bangkok, Thailand, and New York and Los Angeles in the United States, according to studies by the United Nations and others.

More than one-tenth of the world's population, or 643 million people, live in low-lying areas at risk from climate change, say U.S. and European experts. Most imperiled, in descending order, are China, India, Bangladesh, Vietnam, Indonesia, Japan, Egypt, the U.S., Thailand and the Philippines."

Science Of Climate Change

Heidi Cullen

Let analyze step by step position of scientist Heidi Cullen, which she describe in her book: Cullen, Heidi 2010. The Weather of the Future.

She states:

> *(Irish scientist) John Tyndall built a device, called a spectrophotometer, which he used to measure the amount of radiated heat (like the heat radiated from the stove) that gases such as water vapor, carbon dioxide could absorb. His experiment showed that different gases in the atmosphere had different abilities to absorb and transmit heat. Some of the gases in the atmosphere—oxygen, nitrogen, and hydrogen—were essentially transparent to both sunlight and IR, but others gases were in fact opaque: they actually absorbed the IR, as if they were brick in the oven. Those gases include carbon dioxide (CO2) and also methane, nitrous oxide, and water vapor. These greenhouse gases are very good in absorbing infrared light (pages 19–20).*

> *"Carbon dioxide (like other heat-trapping gases, such as methane and water vapor) absorbs the infrared radiation (IR) and warm the air, which in turn warms water below it" (page 20).*

John Tyndall measured how different gases absorb and transmit heat. He did not study the transportation of heat from these gases in the atmosphere. He looked at water vapor as greenhouse gas, and never looked at other properties of water. HE NEVER TRIED TO ESTIMATE CLIMATE CHANGE BECAUSE OF GHG.

Svante Arrhenius (1859–1927)

Arrhenius calculated how much the temperature of the Earth would drop if the amount of CO2 in the atmosphere was halved; he also calculated the temperature increase to be expected from a doubling of CO2 in the atmosphere—arise of about 8º F.

More than a century later, the estimates from state-of-the-art climate models doing the same calculation to determine the increase in temperature due to a doubling of the CO2

concentration show that the calculation by Arrhenius was in the right ballpark. The Fourth Assessment Report of the Intergovernmental Panel on Climate Change (IPCC) synthesized the result from eighteen climate models used by group around the world to estimate climate sensitivity and its uncertainty. They estimate that a doubling of CO2 would lead to an increase in global average temperature of about 5.4º F, with an uncertainty spanning the range from about 3.6º F to 8.1º F (p. 25).

"(Charles David) Keeling (built the gas chromatograph)... and using his Mauna Loa measurements show that with each passing years CO2 levels were steadily moving upward" (p. 28).

"Keeling's record was the icing on the cake, and he rightly stands with Agassiz, Tyndall, and Arrhenius among the giants of climate science" (p. 29).

Of course, Agassiz and Tyndall did the best for their time for science, and neither one blamed GHG for climate change. Arrhenius was the first scientist to use the data of Tyndall to try to calculate what would happen with climate if we double carbon dioxide in the air. He did not look at other phenomena in nature and promote carbon dioxide as the main reason for climate change. Keeling was so obsessed with the importance of carbon dioxide in nature, that he spent all his life on collecting data of the increasing carbon dioxide in the atmosphere.

It is wrong to use second century history of the science of climate change by using Agassiz and Tyndall. It is a mistake of Arrhenius to calculate what happened with climate by doubling the amount of carbon dioxide without looking at the behavior of other gases in nature in full scale of their properties. If Keeling was obsessed with the ideas of Arrhenius it is his fault.

If many of today's scientists of climate change—which are trying to repeat Arrhenius's results with the power of computer calculations—it is their fault. They never analyzed what was wrong in Arrhenius's suggestion and did very large jobs with results which they think are right. It is the biggest mistake in the science of climate change, and no way it's a giant's job as suggest Heidi Cullen. Fortunately, they were wrong.

> *In June 1991, the eruption of Mount Pinatubo in the Philippines provided a perfect natural climate experiment. Pinatubo had injected about 20 million tons of sulfate aerosols into the stratosphere and created the largest clouds of volcanic aerosol haze and the largest perturbation to the stratospheric aerosol layer since the eruption of Krakatau in 1883. The haze spread around the Earth in about three weeks and obtained global coverage after about one year.*

> *Jim Hansen, a leading climate scientist at NASA's Goddard Institute for space studies (GISS) in New York, recognized this as a great opportunity to perform a real time experiment: to use a climate mode to predict how the real world would respond before it actually responded. In other words his team will use the model to make a climate forecast that could be proved correct or incorrect in relatively short time. (p.41, 42).*

Models predict that the planet will cool over the coming year about 0.9ºF globally. The cooling will be concentrated in the Northern Hemisphere and would last about a year.

3

"The result were in, and the climate models were proved correct" (p. 42).

Let's analyze the result.

"Pinatubo had injected about 20 million tons of sulfate aerosols..."

"The haze spread around the Earth in about three weeks and obtained global coverage after about one year."

Sulfate aerosol reflects back to space direct sun radiation. NASA satellites could easily measure the coefficients of reflection to space from the sun radiation. How these coefficients were changed during times after eruption could also be measured. To calculate integral influence during predicted time (one year) it is not so difficult task for computers. The Northern Hemisphere is hotter than its southern counterpart is because in the north, there are more land areas; in the south, there are more oceans. It is not so difficult to predict that the Northern Hemisphere will concentrate its cooling effect, especially if Pinatubo is located in the Northern Hemisphere. The results were in, but sorry, its results do not prove something about climate model.

How smart are scientists with their models?

Eighteen climate models calculated what would happen if carbon dioxide, which trapped infrared radiation, doubled and received 2.25 times differences in their calculation, but in the same direction. Scientists with the same philosophy in mind had Arrhenius changed his hand calculations with the power of computers and received the same result in the same direction. They confirmed only that Arrhenius knew arithmetic. Is it enough to proclaim that the ideas of Arrhenius are right? What would happen if they were to check their models with all properties of water in case of doubled water vapor? Of course, they would receive the same result, at least in direction, because they would look only at one property of water-water vapor as GHG.

"Since Manabe's first experiment with doubled CO2, equilibrium runs have been performed thousands of times using increasingly sophisticated models" (p. 42).

"Whereas Manabe's 1967 model was simply one big grid square meant to cover (the) entire planet, today's climate models have more than 1 million grid square that cover(s) the planet. Each grid square is about 70 miles by 70 miles, with twenty-six vertical layers in the atmosphere" (p. 42).

It is not so important how much smaller the grid will be in the future, it is more important what kind of data we will put in every intersection of the grid. If we put temperature, humidity, pressure, direction and speed of wind, and lots of other data which influences weather conditions, we could receive tendency for climate change.

The question is this: **Which line of these computations supports ideas that carbon dioxide or other GHG are responsible for that?**

You will never find this line, or any combination of lines, in computation. It is up to the scientist's dogma that GHG are responsible for climate change. When they put influence of increasing the amount of carbon dioxide in computer calculations by coefficient, they will receive the same result. But it is illogical to interpret changes in nature by increasing GHG with real changes, which could be by other reasons, but is proportional to the increase of GHG in the atmosphere. Human activities depend on fossil fuel as their main source of energy. These activities not only changed the amount of GHG in the air, but the evaporation of water vapor and reflection of direct sun radiation from arable land as many other influential forces on climate. GHG in the air are only good indicators of these activities. If we change the directions of our activities, we will increase the amount of GHG in nature, but the results could be different.

The most interesting thing that Heidi Cullen wrote about these different directions is that she remembered them, but did not pay enough attention on what another scientists told her. It is strange that scientists, which peer-reviewed her book, somehow missed the opinions of scientists working on other directions.

She wrote about Sahel:

"A semiarid savanna stretching out over 2,400 miles from the Atlantic Ocean in the west and the Red Sea in the east." (p. 63).

"...seasonal rainfall forecasts for the Sahel have been issued since 1997, providing significant help in drought planning and food security...

But although the climate models rely on ocean surface temperature to forecast rainfall and temperature, Gianniny (is a climatologist) is quick to add that h uman activity does still influence the severity of the drought in Sahel"(Cullen, Heidi. 2010. *The Weather of the Future,* 72).

Heidi Cullen wrote about another scientist's opinion—remember it, and did not concentrate on Gianniny's remark about human activities in the Sahel area like land use, deforestation, and overgrazing.

"Of course, there is another broader human influence that goes beyond the behavior of local population. Global warming..." p 72

Another scientist, Chris Reij, thinks that*"human behavior can transform the regional ecology, restore biodiversity, and increase agricultural productivity. Reij thinks that such behavioral changes may even help bring rain in Sahel. "If you put a thermometer into barren, sandy soil you immediately get 120ºF. But just 1 meter away, where you have some surface cover, the temperature immediately drop to 1 09ºF," says Reij. "And with a bit of luck, if you have vast area of regreening, the question is: might that begin to have positive impact on local rainfall as well?" For Reij, this might be the perfect answer."* p 79.

The next scientist from this book is Isaac Held.

"My biggest concern is that the GFDL model turns out to be right," said Held. "If that happens, than sand may have finally won the battle in the Sahel once and for all. Unless, of course, like Reij, we abandon the search for a perfect answer and simply begin to fight back. That must be the biggest Sahelian irony of all" p 80.

The biggest irony for scientists of climate change like Heidi Cullen is that they do not even try to bring more attention to reality, which shows to them scientists like Chris Reij, Gianniny.

Why in the distance of one meter could temperature in soil differ from 120ºF to 109ºF? Is it really changes in the amount of GHG that are so crucial in this case? Or is it the evaporation of water by vegetation which covers or does not cover land in such a close distance? What difference will it be if distances between covered and non-covered land will be 100 m, or 1000 m? Of course, Reij will lose fights to scientists of climate change. Of course, changes by Reij in small areas in Niger's Sahel can't be useful if in millions of other areas in the world it will be the same as a cornfield in Texas, or Virgin Land in Altay, Kazakhstan area, or the Aral Sea. Of course, Heidi Cullen rejects Reij's efforts and after mentioning them, returns to climate model forecasts for July 2015, November 2022, March 2030, January 2050 as the *"perfect answer"* from her side in the herd of majority.

What is this blindness by obsessing with the super power of GHG in nature? Or is it a crime of scientists by obsessing with one idea and claiming that the debate is over? How can scientists of climate change not see that human activities destroy the evaporation of water on continents, on all continents, where we have arable land? It is a riddle and an irony of our time how thousands of scientists could be so blind. They hear about the changing of temperatures by 11ºF over a distance of only 1 m between not cover and cover soil with vegetation and return to business as usual with GHG. How is it possible, Mrs. Heidi Cullen? Sorry that I am so hard on you, but please explain:

"That must be the biggest Sahelian irony of all."

Heidi Cullen at least mentions the opinions of a few scientists, which can see the real world but can't overturn the majority of scientists and their dogma about the role of GHG in the science of climate change.

"Irish scientist John Tyndall built a spectrophotometer to measure amount of radiated heat that gases such as water vapor, carbon dioxide, ozone, methane, nitrous oxide could absorb. These greenhouse gases are very good in absorbing infrared light.

Carbon dioxide (like other heat-trapping gases, such as methane and water vapor) absorbs the infrared radiation and warm the air, which in turn warms water below it."

Dear Heidi, John Tyndall really found that *"Carbon dioxide (like other heat-trapping gases, such as methane and water vapor) absorbs the infrared radiation.* It was your or your's coscientists's suggestion that it will*"warm the air, which in turn warms water below it."* Please try to think: "what will happen to water vapor when it traps infrared radiation?

Why does no one from hundreds of articles about this book even try to criticize your opinion? Is it so difficult to see that water vapor will go up to cloud level, and why it is happening? Is it so difficult to see that parcels of air with water vapor will bring up to the clouds all the gases inside these parcels together with their energy? Is it so difficult to estimate that energy, whose properties of water brings to the cloud level, will escape to space more easily from that level than from ocean (ground) level? Answers to these questions create a different picture for the reason of climate change. Only positive feedback on this book is a shame for the science of climate change and our mass media. The blindness in their minds suppresses any other point of view on the same subject, even in cases when they are written in the book. It is very interesting that all books like this were peer reviewed by many scientists. How editors, friends, readers, etcetera did not see any other possibilities, even in cases when these possibilities were written in the book which they read, I do not know. Are they so busy that they don't have time to understand what they are 'peer reviewing?'

Peer review, at least for the science of climate change, allowed theories to become formal papers without any serious obligation for reviewers. The dogma did not need additional efforts to estimate: "Is it true?" **It is THE DOGMA!** Dogmatic minds are so sure in their estimation that they have only one explanation— GHG. It is enough to mention GHG as the reason for climate change to be a part of dogmatic society of scientists of climate change.

Peer review in researches about climate change became so trivial that everybody, including me, agreed in their necessity. What I read about peer review on Wikipedia was a big surprise for me. It read as follows

Peer review,2012, http://en.wikipedia.org/wiki/Peer_review This page was last modified on 10 April 2012

History

The first recorded editorial prepublication peer-review process was at The Royal Society in 1665 by the founding editor of Philosophical Transactions of the Royal Society, Henry Oldenburg. *In the 20th century, peer review became common for science funding allocations. This process appears to have developed independently from the editorial peer review.*

The first peer-reviewed publication may have been the Medical Essays and Observations published by the Royal Society of Edinburgh*in 1731. The present-day peer-review system evolved from this 18th-century process.*

A professional peer-review process is found in the Ethics of the Physician written by Ishaq bin Ali al-Rahwi (854–931) of al-Raha, Syria. *His work, as well as later Arabic medical manuals, states that a visiting physician must always make duplicate notes of a patient's condition on every visit. When the patient was cured or had died, the notes of the physician were examined by a local medical council of other physicians, who would review the practicing physician's notes to decide whether his/her performance have met the required standards of medical care. If their reviews were negative, the practicing physician could face a*lawsuit*from a maltreated patient.*

Peer review has been a touchstone of modern scientific method *only since the middle of the 20th century, the only exception being* medicine. *Before then, its application was lax in other scientific fields. For example,* Albert Einstein*'s revolutionary* "Annus Mirabilis"papers *in the 1905 issue of* Annalen der Physik*were not peer-reviewed by anyone other than the journal's editor-in-chief,*

Max Planck*(the father of quantum theory), and its co-editor,* Wilhelm Wien. *Although clearly peers (both won Nobel prizes in physics), a formal panel of reviewers was not sought, as is done for many scientific journals today. Established authors and editors were given more latitude in their journalistic discretion, back then. In a recent editorial in Nature, it was stated that "in journals in those days, the burden of proof was generally on the opponents rather than the proponents of new ideas."*

Allegation of bias and suppression

The interposition of editors and reviewers between authors and readers always raises the possibility that the intermediators may serve as gatekeepers. *Some* sociologists of science *argue that peer review makes the ability to publish susceptible to control by* elites*and to personal jealousy. The peer review process may* suppress dissent*against* "mainstream" *theories. Reviewers tend to be especially critical of conclusions that contradict their own views, and lenient towards those that accord with them. At the same time, established scientists are more likely than less established ones to be sought out as referees, particularly by high-prestige journals or* publishers. *As a result, ideas that harmonize with the established experts' are more likely to see print and to appear in premier journals than are iconoclastic or revolutionary ones, which accords with* Thomas Kuhn*'s well-known observations regarding* scientific revolutions.

Peer review failure

Peer review failures occur when a peer-reviewed article contains obvious fundamental errors that undermine at least one of its main conclusions. Many journals have no procedure to deal with peer review failures beyond publishing letters to the editor.

Peer review in scientific journals assumes that the article reviewed has been honestly written, and the process is not designed to detect fraud.

The reviewers usually do not have full access to the data from which the paper has been written and some elements have to be taken on trust. It is not usually practical for the reviewer to reproduce the author's work. Publication of incorrect results does not in itself indicate a peer review failure."

All of that is true; at least I can't publish my articles in magazines and newspapers. I am sure that I am right in my understanding of the main problems, the same as in its solutions, which could be very useful. I was obsessed with my discovery because I saw solutions, which were easy to implement in the USA. I sent them to congressmen, senators, to presidents Bush and Obama and their staff. I also sent them to several universities. I published my book covering by own my expenses and sent it to Michele Obama; it is about the economy and climate change, it is solutions for many domestic and world problem, please take them for free.

In the best cases, I received computer-simulated answers. It is not about me—Albert Einstein, Faraday, and Maxwell may have never been published in today's scientific literature of climate change. Political slogan: "If 98% of scientists support one direction in science, why do we need pay attention to the opinion of the other 2%?" It is easy to proclaim, "The debate is over!" Is it the science of climate change, or is it a sect of people with dogmatic views from blind scientists for blind people?

Andrew Dessler

Let analyze step by step position of scientist Andrew Dessler, which he describe in his book

Dessler, Andrew, 2010 *The Chemistry and Physics of Stratospheric Ozone.*

I am not interested in the chemistry and physics of stratospheric ozone, but I read this book to find something in an area of my interest. I like his next quote:

"Our knowledge of the atmosphere is often incomplete and unknown factors might not only cause the desired outcome to not occur: it might cause the opposite outcome to occur!" p 115.

I also like what I found in his book regarding the height level for clouds.

"The exact temperature at which (Polar stratospheric clouds) PSCs form is a function of pressure and trace gas abundances, but canonical formation temperature, valid near 20 km for typical lower atmospheric condition, is ~196 K. Because of the requirement for such low temperatures, PSCs exist only in the winter and early spring polar regions from tropopause to altitude as high as ~26 km." p 158

"Type I PSCs form from co-condensation of H2 O and HNO3, while type II PSCs form from condensation of water vapor." p 187.

It is also confirms that water vapor could be even higher.

Let step by step analyze another book, which Dessler wrote together with another scientist Parson.

Dessler, Andrew; Parson, Edward, 2010, The science and politics of global climate change.

> *What is climate?*
>
> *The climate of a place, a region, or the Earth as a whole, is the average over time of the meteorological condition that occurs there—the average weather. For example, in the month of November between 1971 and 2000, the average daily high temperature in Washington, DC was 14ºC, the average daily low was 1ºC and 0.3 cm of precipitation fell. These average values, along with averages of other meteorological quantities such as humidity, wind speed, cloudiness, and snow and ice coverage, define the November climate of Washington over this period. p 7.*

Please, pay attention: the average daily high temperature, the average daily low temperature, precipitation, averages of other meteorological quantities such as humidity, wind speed, cloudiness, and snow and ice coverage... Exactly these averages scientists are putting into computers for computation in the computer's models.

Electromagnetic radiation

The source of energy for the Earth's climate is sunlight, which is a form of electromagnetic radiation."

Most photons emitted by the Sun have wavelength between about 0.3 and 0.8 microns. This is also the range of wavelength that are visible to human eyes.Photons with longer wavelengths, beyond red, are called infrared and are not visible to humans.As an object's temperature increases, the amount of energy it emits as blackbody radiation increases. The relation between temperature and total radiated energy, known as Stefan-Boltzman Law, states that energy emitted is proportional to the fourth power of temperature.

"A BLACK BODY IS AN IDEALIZED OBJECT THAT ABSORBS ALL PHOTONS THAT FALL ON IT, AND EMIT photons with wavelength, that are determined by its temperature. pages 8,9.

Please, try to remember that energy emitted by black body is proportional to the fourth power of temperature. The Earth is not a black body, but the surface of any part of the Earth will emit energy close to the Stefan-Boltzman Law—proportional to the fourth power of temperature. The highest temperature on the Earth is 70.7ºC and the lowest temperature is -89.2ºC, or in Kelvin scale, it will be 343.85ºK and 183.95ºK. It means that Earth can't be looked at as one body. Different regions of Earth will emit different amounts of energy *"that are determined by its temperature."* If wind transports heat from hotter places to cooler, the process will cool hot places and heat cool places. Average temperature must be the same as before the transportation of energy. Emitted energy

"is proportional to the fourth power of temperature."

In result, common emitted energy after the transportation of heat will be less for these two areas. It will happen because the temperature of a hot place will reduce amount of emission and emissions depending on the fourth power of temperature will play the biggest role in this process. Transportation of heat from the Equator to the poles will reduce integral emissions of heat from the Earth and, as a result, will bring global warming according to the Stefan-Boltzman Law.

It means that today by the science of climate change measuring average temperatures on the Earth is fooling itself. If there will be less transfer of heat from the Equator to the poles, average temperatures could be the same, but integral energy emissions to space from the Earth will be bigger. In result, it will be global cooling.

Global warming, global cooling, or climate change are misleading terms that do not underline the real reasons and possibilities of disaster. In future I will use terminology, using by scientists for simplicity to reply on their points, but, please, try to remember my point.

Any transfer of energy from the Equator to the poles will help melt ice in Greenland, Antarctica, and other mountainous areas, which in result, brings more dangerous changes in ocean levels. To better understand this point, please imagine the Earth without any continents and only one ocean with an equal depth of water. Of course, evaporation in the Equatorial area will be bigger than in areas closer to the poles, but it will be more stable climate all around the globe with less powerful hurricanes and other unstable conditions. Only continents between the oceans are responsible for today's instabilities. Different evaporation from the same area in continent and ocean create huge convection forces on continent and ocean breezes, which are result of these convection forces. Our strategy in climate change must be to make any transfers of energy from the Equator to the poles as less as possible. In the case of global cooling, our strategy must be the same—keep heat close to the Equator. It will increase areas which are good for living, even in global cooling conditions.

"Feedback and climate sensitivity

Even the simplest models, show that the Earth surface must warm, if the amount of CO2 or other infrared-absorbing gases in the atmosphere is increased."

I have several problems with this statement. It must be explained how the amount of CO2 influence climate in model. If it only by coefficient of increasing amount of *CO2* in atmosphere it is not enough to explain all processes in reality. Reality is far away from mechanical sum of different factors. If you will put in a computer model *"the average daily high temperature, the average daily low temperature, precipitation, averages of other meteorological quantities such as humidity, wind speed, cloudiness, and snow and ice coverage..."*Please show me that exactly CO2 is responsible for the claim that the Earth's surface must warm. Here we have another possibility. Knowing the amount of CO2 that was increased, perhaps from 280 ppm to 350 ppm, we could put the forcing factor 350/280=1.25, but it is up to the scientist who did that to say that the increasing of GHG is a forcing factor for climate change. The computer model does not show how exactly CO2 influences climate, especially if in reality other gases will diminish heating effect of carbon dioxide. If changes in the average temperature on the Earth are proportional to this forcing factor (1.25), it is not enough to blame GHG for these changes. Maybe I am wrong. Please, correct me in this case.

"As the climate warms in response to the increased CO2 , many others (sic) things change.

Most importantly, as the atmosphere warms it holds more water vapor. Since water vapor is also a greenhouse gas, this caused additional warming, Such knock-on effects of increased CO2— additional changes caused by the initial change—are called feedback, and are responsible for much of the warming caused by increasing greenhouse gases.

Water vapor is the most powerful feedback, capable of doubling the warming caused by CO2 alone, but many others feedback are also important in the climate system."

How is it good to unite water vapor and carbon dioxide in this case? Let's imagine the Earth's atmosphere without water vapor and methane. Greenhouse gases like carbon dioxide (CO_2) and nitrous oxide (N_2O) will fill the air, and because they are heavier than oxygen and nitrogen, only a slow process of Brownian motion will mix the air. It will keep these GHG mostly close to the source of their origin—the surface of the Earth. In this case, the theory of the influence of greenhouse gases on the climate will be without any doubt. Only light gases like water vapor and methane change this situation simultaneously. Any parcel of air with water vapor or methane will make this parcel lighter and, like in balloon, will move that parcel UP to cloud level. It is a completely different picture, which for some reason is out of mind for scientists.

"Another example involves melting ice, as the climate warms, mostly in glaciers and the Oceans near the Poles. Ice is highly reflective, and the land or water exposed when ice melts are darker. Consequently, a reflection in ice increases the fraction of incoming solar energy absorbed by the Earth's surface, also causing further warming."

There is nothing wrong in these statements.

"The water-vapor feedback and the ice feedback are both examples of positive feedbacks—feedbacks that amplify an initial warming."

This is a beginning of a huge mistake—water vapor and other properties of water are helping all gases to reach clouds level and release their energy there. They can't create positive feedback and authors of this book even show it in next statements:

"There are also negative feedbacks, by which the initial warming causes changes that produce cooling. For example, the temperatures of the surface and upper atmosphere are linked by vertical mixing from thunderstorms: as the surface warms, so does the upper atmosphere. Since a warmer atmosphere radiates more energy into space, this effect will offset some of the warming caused by increased greenhouse gases." pages 16–17.

It is a very interesting statement: *"Since a warmer atmosphere radiates more energy into space, this effect will offset some of the warming...*" Is there no vertical mixing of atmosphere by all the vertical movements of water vapor, which during few hours we could see in clouds? Does latent heat from the condensation of water vapor in the upper troposphere not heat the air there? If air is heated by the heat of condensation on the cloud level, it will radiate more energy to space as suggested by the authors. Are only clouds in thunderstorms coming to the upper atmosphere? Will there be a movement of water vapor UP, even in the case of a blue sky? Will this movement by condensation warm the upper atmosphere? Will "*a warmer atmosphere radiates more energy into space*" in this case? Of course thunderstorms are more powerful in transporting energy to the upper atmosphere, but even in the case of the biggest thunderstorm's area, they cover hundreds of times less than all the surface of the Earth. The same could be said about time for thunderstorms, which is a hundred times shorter than more peaceful weather conditions, which we see all around the globe. And exactly in these 'peaceful' weather conditions is where the most evaporation of water occurs, and water vapor is going up all around the world. Most condensation occurs in the upper troposphere, which releases heat there and more energy will be radiated to space, according to authors. This phenomenon was discovered in the nineteenth century and authors correctly understand its meaning, unfortunately, only in the case of thunderstorms. After that, they returned to completely forgetting about the influence of the properties of water on climate:

"*As the climate warms in response to the increased CO2...*"

Scientist Tyndall checked that carbon dioxide really trapped IR radiation, but to claim that climate warms right now by increasing the amount of CO2 in the air is not a correct statement. It is only a suggestion without any significant scientific proof. Scientist Tyndall also checked that water vapor also trapped IR radiation. At the same time, it is wrong statement from the scientists of climate change: "*The water-vapor feedback and the ice feedback are both examples of positive feedbacks – feedbacks that amplify an initial warming.*" This is, I'm sorry, speculation without any confirmation. Water vapor together with others properties of water actually cooling the atmosphere.

Ice feedback by reflection of direct sun radiation and water vapor by increasing "trapping" effects of GHG CAN'T BE MENTIONED WITHOUT ANALYSIS OF OTHER PROPERTIES OF WATER.

No one computer model could confirm that carbon dioxide and water vapor would influence the warming effect of today's level. Please remember what scientist Chris Reij said about the 11ºF difference of temperature in cover by vegetation and not cover by them land with a distance from each other of only 1 m.

"Climate models and weather models.

> *Global Climate Models or GCMs-mathematical representations of the Earth that run on computers. These models represent the known physical laws that governs the behavior of the climate system—such as conservation of energy, momentum and mass—as well as evaporation of surface water, condensation of water in the atmosphere to form clouds, and many others physical processes and feedbacks. To provide accurate representations of the climate, GCMs must also represent the behavior of other parts of the Earth that interact with the climate, including the oceans, the land surface, the cryosphere (surface ice), and the biosphere (the world's ecosystems).*

> *The biggest challenge to produce an accurate GCM comes from the vast range of spatial scales at which atmospheric processes operate— from pressure system of thousands of kilometers, to a clouds of a few kilometers, to turbulent eddies of a few meters, tomolecular activity of millionths or even billionths of a meter. Models must divide the atmosphere into finite sized grid-cells, which are the smallest units for which they explicitly define and calculate atmospheric properties."*

If Global Climate Models used " *physical laws that governs the behavior of the climate system—such as conservation of energy, momentum and mass—as well as evaporation of surface water, condensation of water in the atmosphere to form clouds"*only as parameters in this model it is not enough. Evaporation process cool air, the same as condensation released energy, which heat the air. If scientist can't put in computer behavior of parcels of air by cooling and heating process, their models are useless. Every small object, perhaps car on the grass could create small parcel of air, heated by the hot roof of car (in sunny day), which will create movement of this parcel UP. It is impossible to predict and put in computer models behavior of millions and millions of this kind of subject, which integral influence could bring in real life opposite influence on climate, than models predict.

Please pay attention:

"Models must divide the atmosphere into finite sized grid-cells, which are the smallest units for which they explicitly define and calculate atmospheric properties."

Only on these small units do models *"explicitly define and calculate atmospheric properties."*

"Present computing speeds limit the smallest atmospheric grid-cells to about 100 kilometers horizontally, sliced into vertical layers about one kilometer thick. Processes operating at smaller scales than this, such as clouds, cannot be represented explicitly in the models but must instead be parameterized."

Again, we have an interesting statement:

"Processes operating at smaller scales than this, such as clouds, cannot be represented explicitly in the models but must instead be parameterized."

It means that we put into the computer some parameters FROM ONE PLACE with an area of 100 km x 100 km.

"Parameterization means representing the effects of these smaller-scale processes as function of variables the models does explicitly resolve, such as temperature and water vapor. So while GCMs cannot represent individual clouds, which are much smaller than a single grid-cell, they can estimate the average cloudiness of a cell as a function of the cell relative humidity and winds."

This is a very interesting statement:

"So while GCMs cannot represent individual clouds, which are much smaller than a single grid-cell, they can estimate the average cloudiness of a cell as a

function of the cell relative humidity and winds."

Humidity and wind help estimate average cloudiness. How does water vapor behave from ground (ocean) level to the upper troposphere? How does water vapor behave above the upper troposphere? How does the process of cloud formation change the behavior of water vapor in the atmosphere? All of these questions are beyond the parameterization process *"as evaporation of surface water, condensation of water in the atmosphere to form clouds, and many others physical processes."*

"Parameterizations are highly diverse. Some have well-founded physical bases, while others, are ad hoc constructions that let the model produce a realistic present day climate. Consequently, parameterizations are one of the largest sources of uncertainty in GCMs."

Please, pay attention:

"... parameterizations are one of the largest sources of uncertainty in GCMs."

Thank you, Mr. Dessler; you confirm that parameterizations are one of the largest sources of uncertainty in GCMs.

"GCMs can be tested by examining how well they reproduce the Earth's actual climate." pages 17, 18.

"Increased climate forcing from human activities."

"The most important increase has been CO2."

"Methane (CH4)"

"Nitrous oxide (N2 O)"

"Chlorofluorocarbons (CFCs)" p 20.

All gases in this book are forcing factors for climate change only because they all trap infrared radiation. In my opinion, it is not enough. The behavior of different gases in the atmosphere are different, at least because of their molecular weight. Methane and water vapor can't be in the same position as carbon dioxide and nitrous oxide. As lighter gases, they are playing different roles in nature than heavier gases, despite all of them trapping infrared radiation. It is a huge mistake. Unfortunately, their differences are not underscored in today's science of climate change. It is better to say that today's science of climate change ignores these differences.

Here is next very interesting information we found in this book:

"... a record of temperature and CO2 for the Antarctic region... constructed from ice cores. This record shows much more fine-grained detail... including the shape of ice-age cycles with relatively short, warm interglacials (lasting 10,000-30,000 years) separating long, cold ice ages (lasting ~ 100,000 years)." Note also that ice ages are only 5-8º C colder than today— a seemingly small difference considering the Earth is essentially a different planet during an ice age, with glaciers several thousands feet thick covering much of North America, sea level 300 feet lower than today, and all of the others accompanying changes in the world environment and ecosystems."

I can't understand why scientists are looking at the correlation between temperature and carbon dioxide and trying to prove something. If we know that cold water has more carbon dioxide than hot water and that every hot period began with the melting of ice, then that explanation is good enough for this correlation. The increase or decrease of the amount of carbon dioxide is caused by temperature.

IT IS NOT TEMPERATURE THAT IS INCREASED OR DECREASED BECAUSE OF CARBON DIOXIDE!

"The cooling into an ice age is slow, taking several tens of thousands of years, while the warming at the end of an ice age occurs faster, in about 10,000 years."

We know that to melt 1 kg of ice we need 80Kcal of energy. When water is frosting to ice, it will release the same 80Kcal of energy.

What is the difference?

In my opinion, the difference is in releasing heat, which decreases the frosting process and increase it timing. The difference is in the reflection of direct sun radiation by surfaces of water and ice. Even before the Industrial Revolution, the eruption of volcano occurred and produced dust. Even in glacier period close to equator were areas without glaciers. Dust from these areas and from volcano eruption covered all surface of the Earth, including all glacier.

All of these, and maybe many other sources of dust, cover ice and reduce the reflection of direct sun radiation. We also know that before the cooling-period, oceans take more area of the Earth than they do after the maximum of cooling. Reflection of direct sun radiation from the ocean is always less than that from even dirty ice. It helps heat the atmosphere and also slow process of frosting, making cooling of the Earth longer. In the case of the cooling period, new ice is also covered constantly by snow, which increases the reflection of direct sun radiation. . Process of cooling became faster if more area of the Earth's surface covered by glaciers. In other words, cooling must be a very slow process in the beginning of the cooling period (oceans reflect less direct sun radiation) and after that the speed of cooling must increase (ice increases the reflection of direct sun radiation). In the case of warming, every melting layer of ice covered by dust brings this dust onto the next layer of melting ice. As a result, all glaciers will reflect less and less direct sun radiation back to space. More energy will stay on the Earth's surface and warming will be faster and faster. More simple reasons could explain the speed of cooling and warming than the decreasing and increasing amount of carbon dioxide in air.

"We can also say with high confidence, however, that the last few decades of the twentieth century are warmer than any comparable period over the

last 400 years, and possibly even warmer than the peak of the medieval worm period, around 1,000 years ago." pages 78-80.

Scientist Dessler explains this warming in our days only by increasing the amount of GHG emitted by mankind activities.

I can only repeat what I wrote before:

"A corn crop dries in a field on July 28, 2011 near Perriton Texas...

Drought in Zimbabwe...

Erosion of Virgin Land...

Shrinking of the Aral Sea...'

All are the result of human activities, the same as in many other places on all continents. All of these activities, of course, increase the amount of GHG in the atmosphere. At the same time, it is impossible for nature to be so precise in response. It is the main argument against GHG theory." Please remember what scientist Chris Reij said about 11ºF difference of temperature in cover by vegetation and not cover by them land on distance from each other only 1 m.

James Hansen

Let find, what Wikipedia is writing about James Hansen and step by step analyze this article.

James Hansen, http://en.wikipedia.org/wiki/James_Hansen This page was last modified on 7 April 2012.

> *"NASA* **GISS***: NASA* **Goddard Institute fo***r space study.*
>
> *The first GISS global temperature analysis was published in 1981. Hansen and his co-author analyzed the surface air temperature at meteorological stations focusing on the years from 1880 to 1985. Temperatures for stations closer together than 1000 kilometers were shown to be highly correlated, especially in the mid-latitudes, which*

provided a way to combine the station data to provide accurate long-term variations. They conclude that global mean temperatures can be determined even though meteorological stations are typically in the Northern hemisphere and confined to continental regions. Warming in the past century was found to be 0.5–0.7 °C, with warming similar in both hemispheres. When the analysis was updated in 1988, the four warmest years on record were all in the 1980s. The two warmest years were 1981 and 1987."

It is very difficult to imagine that data from stations closer together than 1000 kilometers could be correlated enough to find warming from the past century to be 0.5–0.7 °C. Is it that these stations absolutely do not depend on condition of the land around the stations? Do close forests, rivers, lakes, farmer's fields, etc. not influence data in different conditions of wind directions, speed, etc.?

Thank you for the information that *"meteorological stations are typically in the Northern hemisphere and confined to continental regions."* It is a really reliable computation. NOTE MY SARCASM ABOUT THEM. How could scientist Chris Reij find 11ºF difference of temperature in cover by vegetation and not cover by vegetation land with a distance from each other of only 1 m? Please do not forget that he measured the temperature of the land, not the air. Here we have a distance of around 1000 kilometers and the data is still correlated? Let us forget about forests, lakes, cornfields, rivers, semiarid areas, or mounts. What about oceans without stations?

With the 1991 eruption of Mount Pinatubo, 1992 saw a cooling in the global temperatures. There was speculation that this would cause the next couple years to be cooler because of the large <u>serial correlation</u> in the global temperatures. Bassett and Lin found the statistical odds of a new temperature record to be small. Hansen countered by saying that having insider information shifts the odds to those that know the physics of the climate system, and that whether there is a new temperature record depends upon the particular data set used.

The temperature data was updated in 1999 to report that 1998 was the warmest year since the instrumental data began in 1880. They also found that the rate of temperature change was larger than any time in instrument history, and conclude that the recent El Nino was not totally responsible for the large temperature anomaly in 1998. In spite of this, the United States had seen a smaller degree of warming, and a region in the eastern U.S. and the western Atlantic Ocean had actually cooled slightly.

What kind of insider information could explain why the*"United States had seen a smaller degree of warming, and a region in the eastern U.S. and the western Atlantic Ocean had actually cooled slightly?"* And if so, how is it possible that *"Temperatures for stations closer together than 1000 kilometers were shown to be highly correlated..."* At least I did not read any explanation from these facts.

"2001 saw a major update to how the temperature was calculated. It incorporated corrections due to the following reasons: time-of-observation bias, station history changes, classification of rural/urban stations, the urban adjustment based on satellite measurements of night light intensity, and relying more on rural station than urban. Evidence was found of local urban warming in urban, suburban and small-town records."

It is a very good direction but, in my opinion, it is not enough. We must check the position of stations also to constantly changing environments, like forest, field, lake, river, influence of tilling the land, growing and watering crops, their vegetation period, etc. If scientists of climate change ignore facts, which is familiar to scientists like Gianniny and Chris Reij, their ignorance puts down all the science of climate change. They are using data without any thoughts about the real reasons. They have only one trump in mind—GHG.

"The anomalously high global temperature in 1998 due to <u>El Niño</u> *resulted in a brief drop in subsequent years. However, a 2001 Hansen report in the journal Science states that global warming continues, and that the increasing temperatures should stimulate discussions on how to slow global warming. The temperature data*

was updated in 2006 to report that temperatures are now 0.8 °C warmer than a century ago, and conclude that the recent global warming is a real climate change and not an artifact from the <u>urban heat island effect</u> . The regional variation of warming, with more warming in the higher latitudes, is further evidence of warming that is anthropogenic in origin."

Why is more warming in the higher latitude evidence of human influence in warming?

"In 2007, <u>Stephen McIntyre</u> notified <u>GISS</u> that many of the U.S. temperature records from the Historical Climatology Network (USHCN) displayed a discontinuity around the year 2000. NASA corrected the computer code used to process the data and credited McIntyre with pointing out the flaw.Hansen indicated that he felt that several news organizations had overreacted to this mistake.In 2010, Hansen published a paper entitled 'Global Surface Temperature Change' describing current global temperature analysis."

I am not overreacting; I understand the difficulties of collecting data and correcting them from the urban heat island effect. I agree that global warming is anthropological in origin. In my opinion, Hansen, as any scientist must admit, we have not *"this mistake,"*but many mistakes in methodology and analysis, which brings all the achievements of the science of climate change to zero.

"Black carbon

Hansen has also contributed toward the understanding of <u>black carbon</u>on regional climate. In recent decades, northern China has experienced increased drought, and southern China has received increased summer rain resulting in a larger number of floods. Southern China has had a decrease in temperatures while most of the world has warmed. In a paper with Menon and colleagues, through the use of observations and climate models results, they conclude that the black carbon heats the air, increases convection and precipitation, and leads to larger surface cooling than if the aerosols were sulfates."

It is remarkable that"*the black carbon heats the air, increases convection and precipitation, and leads to larger surface cooling than if the aerosols were sulfates.*"

I can't understand why scientists wrote about these phenomena and did not make a bigger conclusion. If black carbon heats the air because it takes direct sun radiation, it must be HOTTER.

DESPITE THIS HOTTER AIR, WE HAVE A COOLING EFFECT BY INCREASING CONVECTION AND PRECIPITATION.

Thank you, scientists Hansen, Menon, and colleagues. You confirm the point that during the last seven years I have badly been trying to bring to the attention of all science communities, newspapers, scientific and not-so-scientific journals and magazines, congressmen, senators, and even two presidents—Bush and Obama, as well as their staff.

A huge region of southern China was COOLED! IT WAS COOLED DESPITE THAT THERE MUST BE MORE CARBON DIOXIDE AND BLACK CARBON THAN IN MANY OTHER AREAS.

It was cooled "*while most of the world has warmed.*" Why did it happen?

Scientists honestly answer this question as "*black carbon heats the air, increases convection and precipitation, and leads to larger surface cooling than if the aerosols were sulfates.*"

Why do they forget about the cooling effect of convection and precipitation in their future analysis?

"*Dangerous anthropogenic interference*

The United Nations Framework Convention on Climate Change *is an international environmental treaty that was aimed at stabilizing greenhouse gas concentrations in the atmosphere at a level that would prevent dangerous anthropogenic interference with the climate system.*

In 2003 Hansen wrote a paper called Can We Defuse the Global Warming Time Bomb? where he argues that human-caused forces on the climate are now greater than natural ones, and that this, over a long time period, can cause large climate changes.He further states that a lower limit on "dangerous anthropogenic interference" is set by the stability of the Greenland and Antarctic <u>ice sheets</u>. His view on actions to mitigate climate change is that "halting global warming requires urgent, unprecedented international cooperation, but the needed actions are feasible and have additional benefits for human health, agriculture and the environment."

Here we can see how dangerous today's science of climate change could be for the entire world.

"In a 2004 presentation at the University of Iowa, Hansen announced that he was told by high-ranking government officials not to talk about how anthropogenic influence could have a dangerous effect on climate because it's not understood what dangerous means, or how human are actually affecting climate. He describes this as a <u>Faustian bargain</u> because atmospheric aerosols have health risks, and should be reduced, but doing so will effectively increase the warming effects from CO2."

If GHG do not play such a huge role in nature, as most scientists suggest, efforts by the United Nations to lower the limit on *"dangerous anthropogenic interference"*will bring more harm than good. Most important in this case is that we will lose time to make changes, which really could bring results.

"Hansen and coauthors propose that the global mean temperature is a good tool to diagnose dangerous anthropogenic interference with the climate system."

This statement contradicts with the previous statement that *"the regional variation of warming, with more warming in the higher latitudes, is further evidence of warming that is anthropogenic in origin."*

The danger is the increasing temperature in the higher latitude, which will melt ice in Greenland and Antarctica.

"Two elements are particularly important when discussing dangerous anthropogenic interference: sea level rise and the extinction of species. They describe a business as usual scenario, which has greenhouse gases growing at approximately 2% per year, and an alternate scenario, in which greenhouse gases concentrations decline. Under the alternate scenario, sea levels could rise by 1 meter per century, causing problems due to the dense population in coastal areas. But this would be minor compared to the 10 meter increase in sea level under the business as usual scenario. Hansen describes the situation with species extinction similarly to sea level rise. Assuming the alternate scenario, the situation is not good, but it is much worse for business as usual".

Obsession with carbon dioxide brings, without any doubt, great scientists, like Hansen, to the ABSOLUTELY WRONG DIRECTION. HUGE EFFORTS WHICH WORLD GOVERNMENTS AND POPULATIONS WILL SPEND IN THE WRONG DIRECTION WILL BRING THE OPPOSITE EFFECT!

It is good to repeat what scientist Andrew Dessler wrote:

"Our knowledge of the atmosphere is often incomplete and unknown factors might not only cause the desired outcome to not occur: it might cause the opposite outcome to occur!"

If GHG does not play a main role in nature, we will receive from recommendations of scientists of climate change exactly the opposite outcome.

"The concept of dangerous anthropogenic interference was clarified in a 2007 paper. They find that further warming of 1 °C would be highly disruptive to humans. An alternative scenario would keep the warming to below this if climate sensitivity were below 3 °C for doubled CO2. The conclusion is that CO2 levels above 450 ppm are considered dangerous, but that reduction in non-CO2 greenhouse gases can provide temporary relief from drastic CO2 cuts. Further, they find that arctic climate change has been forced by non-CO2 constituents as much as CO2. They caution that prompt

action is needed to slow CO2 growth and prevent a dangerous anthropogenic interference."

Anthropogenic influence plus influence of wrong scientific points about GHG, of course, will bring a catastrophic situation on Earth. Every scientist has the right to make mistakes, but why are thousands of scientists making the same mistake? Is the discipline in science the same as in the Army? Even soldiers who don't have their own thoughts are bad soldiers.

"Climate model development and projections

Vilhelm Bjerknesbegan the modern development of the general circulation model in the early 20th century. The progress of numerical modeling was slow due to the slow speed of early computers and the lack of adequate observations. It wasn't until the 1950s that the numerical models were getting close to being realistic. Hansen's first contribution to numerical climate models came with the 1974 publication of the GISS model. He and his colleagues claimed that the model was successful in simulating the major features of sea-level pressure and 500mb heights in the North American region.

A 1981 Science publication by Hansen and a team of scientists at Goddard concluded that carbon dioxide in the atmosphere would lead to warming sooner than previously predicted. They used a one-dimensional radiative-convective model that calculates temperature as a function of height. They reported that the results from the 1D model are similar to the more complex 3D models, and can simulate basic mechanisms and feedbacks. Hansen predicted that temperatures would rise out of the climate noise by the 1990s, much earlier than predicted by other researches. He also predicted that it would be difficult to convince politicians and the public to react.

We are lucky that in the United States skeptical minds to climate change prevail. The main problems regarding the economy for the Obama administration are created by the scientists of climate change. These scientists are not only wrong that GHG are responsible for climate change, but they also recommend the wrong engineering solutions to fight climate change. Windmills, solar cells, nuclear power plants, these are as disastrous for the environment as they are for the world economy.

"By the early 1980s the computational speed of computers, along with refinements in climate models, allowed longer experiments. The models now included physics beyond the previous equations, such as convection schemes, diurnal changes, and snow depth calculations. The advances in computational efficiency, combined with the added physics, meant the GISS model I could be run for five years. They showed that global climate can be simulated reasonably well with a grid-point resolution as coarse as 1000 kilometers.

The first climate prediction computed from a general circulation model that was published by Hansen was in 1988, the same year as his well-known Senate testimony. It used the second generation of the GISS model to estimate the change in mean surface temperature based on a variety of scenarios of future greenhouse gas emissions. Hansen concluded that global warming would be evident within the next few decades, and that it would result in temperatures at least as high as during the <u>Eemian</u>. *He argued that, if the temperature rises 0.4 °C above the 1950-1980 mean for a few years, it is the "smoking gun" pointing to human-caused global warming.*

Please Google Richard Lindzen. I do not completely agree with this scientist, but he was almost alone against all scientists, which emphasize the influence of GHG in nature. These scientists, together with Al Gore, bring to the science of climate change the biggest damage in the history of science, which still has not been realized in the world. Please read the articles by this scientist that voice his opinions about the "science of fear" and Al Gore. I am sure that he deserves your attention.

"A year later, he joined with <u>Rahmstorf</u> *and colleagues comparing climate projections with observations. The comparison is done from 1990 through January 2007 against physics-based models that are independent from the observations after 1990. They show that the climate system may be responding faster than the models indicate. Rahmstorf and coauthors show concern that sea levels are rising at*

the high range of the IPCC projections, and that it is due to thermal expansion and not from the Greenland or Antarctic ice sheets.

Following the launch of spacecraft capable of determining temperatures, <u>Roy Spencer</u> and <u>John Christy</u> published the first version of their <u>satellite temperature measurements</u> in 1990. Contrary to climate models and surface measurements, their results showed a cooling in the<u>troposphere</u>. In 1998, Wentz and Schabel determined that orbital decay had an effect on the derived temperatures. Hansen compared the corrected troposphere temperatures with the results of the published GISS model, and concluded that the model is in good agreement with the observations, noting that the satellite temperature data had been the last holdout of , and that the correction of the data would result in a change from discussing whether global warming was occurring to what is the rate of global warming, and what should be done about it."

We must agree that *"global warming was occurring."* At the same time we must understand that global warming, cooling, climate change are misleading terminology. Most dangerous is rising level of oceans. What should be done about it? Scientists which blame carbon dioxide and other GHG for climate change will bring the wrong advice to try to answer their own question! Their advice to governments in the world will be more dangerous than the position of a *"global warming denialist."* *"Denialists"* at least will not call for directions that will mostly harm the environment. By naming other sides as *"denialists"* instead of analyzing their point of view only shows that it is mostly a political game rather than real science in the minds of scientists of climate change. Without an answer to the question: "What are the real reasons for climate change?" all recommendations by scientists to governments in the world are wrong and dangerous. We must again and again check and recheck their reasoning.

Let analyze statement from article

Hansen, J., Mki. Sato, R. Ruedy, K. Lo, D.W. Lea, and M. Medina-Elizade (2006), Global temperature change:

"Global surface temperature has increased 0.2°C per decade in the past 30 years, similar to the warming rate predicted in the 1980s in initial global climate model simulations with transient greenhouse gas changes. Warming is larger in the Western Equatorial Pacific than in the Eastern Equatorial Pacific over the past century, and we suggest that the increased West–East temperature gradient may have increased the likelihood of strong El Niños, such as those of 1983 and 1998. Comparison of measured sea surface temperatures in the Western Pacific with paleoclimate data suggests that this critical ocean region, and probably the planet as a whole, is approximately as warm now as at the Holocene maximum and within 1°C of the maximum temperature of the past million years.

We conclude that global warming of more than 1°C, relative to 2000, will constitute "dangerous" climate change as judged from likely effects on sea level and extermination of species"

If we look at GHG as an indicator of human activities, which changed situation on continents proportionally to energy used by mankind to make these changes, we must reevaluate the reasons to what happened in Holocene and other periods in the history of the Earth. In this case, we must look at the amount of carbon dioxide in ice in Holocene and others periods completely different than scientists are estimating and analyzing right now. It is a very difficult task, but these studies could bring an absolutely new view on the climate history of the Earth. Situations today could be more dangerous than even James Hansen predicted, but the evaluation of changes on our planet could bring solutions to fight back not only global warming, but global cooling as well—which will definitely be soon on the Earth and we must start preparing for these changes in both directions.

Let analyze next article:

Hansen, J., R. Ruedy, M. Sato, and K. Lo (2010), Global surface temperature change,

GISS analyses beginning with Hansen et al. [1999] *include a homogeneity adjustment to minimize local (nonclimatic) anthropogenic effects on measured temperature change. Such effects* *are usually largest in urban locations where buildings and energy use often cause a warming bias. Local anthropogenic cooling can also occur, for example, from irrigation and planting of vegetation [Oke, 1989], but on average, these effects are probably outweighed by urban warming (.*

It is again a riddle for me that Hansen agrees that *"local anthropogenic cooling can also occur, for example, from irrigation and planting of vegetation"*and throw away this point. At the same time in USA in 2000, harvested area only for grain was 282.1 million acres.

Crop	Harvested Area (million acres)	Cash Receipts from Sales ($ billion)
Corn (grain)	72.7	15.1
Soybeans	72.7	12.5
Hay	59.9	3.4
Wheat	53.0	5.5
Cotton	13.1	4.6
Sorghum (grain)	7.7	0.82
Rice	3.0	

It is interesting to calculate from this table that the amount of cash received in this case was in the $ billion —41.92.

At the same time, theWashington Post with Bloomberg Business ran a headline stating: *'Iran saber rattling over oil that the energy crisis is still with us.'* The report from February of 2012 also stated that

"in 2011, the United States <u>paid a net of $326.5 billion for oil imports,</u> *accounting for 44 percent of the U.S. trade deficit."*

It is very strange that we received from 279.1 million acres of land (minus 3.0 for rice) eight times less cash than we spent for oil. (Please, remember this fact.)

I can't understand how the effect of 282.1 million acres of arable land could be outweighed by urban warming? Does irrigation occur during the whole year? Are these huge areas only cooling during the year? If Hansen and his team were not obsessed with GHG theory, of course, they could pay attention and closely look at all questions surrounding human activities on the land. Of course, they have possibilities to solve these complex influences on climate by fields, deforestation, and many other influential forces which mankind activities caused and are causing in nature.

Only why do they need to do these jobs?

They have predictable coefficients of the growing amount of GHG in nature, which is easy to put into a computer. Populations willingly will swallow GHGs theory as the main reason for climate change. Millions of articles do their jobs to stop readers from real evaluation of *"the most dangerous and scientifically proved* (sic) *enemies of mankind—GHG."*

I prefer to think that the enemies of mankind are scientists which think that GHG are *"the most dangerous and scientifically proved* (sic) *enemies."* With the best wishes for mankind, their blindness will bring the biggest damage to our civilization.

> *"...the global surface temperatureanomalies for the past 4 decades, relative to the 1951–1980 base period. On average, successive decades warmed by 0.17°C. The warming of the 1990s (0.13°C relative to the 1980s) was reduced by the temporary effect of the 1991 Mount Pinatubo volcanic eruption. (El Chichon, in the prior decade, produced a global average aerosol optical depth only about half as large as Pinatubo.)*
>
> *Warming in these recent decades is larger over land than over ocean, as expected for a forced climate change, in part because the ocean responds more slowly than the land because of the ocean's large thermal inertia."*

It must be clear how large the ocean's thermal inertia is. Is it one year, ten years, or more? If authors mention *'in part,'* it will be good to declare the other part or parts.

"Warming during the past decade is enhanced, relative to the global mean warming, by about 50% in the United States, a factor of 2–3 in Eurasia, and a factor of 3–4 in the Arctic and the Antarctic Peninsula."

Why in the USA does only 50% of global mean warming? Why is it 4–6 times bigger in Eurasia, and 6–8 times in the Arctic and Antarctic Peninsula? Is it meant that ocean's thermal inertia for some reason is working in Indian, Pacific, and Atlantic oceans till some latitude and for some reason stops working closer to the poles? Or are all of these words, that are without any scientific meaning, going to be swallowed by readers which stop thinking about the thousands of times that pseudo information is repeated?

"Warming of the ocean surface has been largest over the Arctic Ocean, second largest over the Indian and western Pacific oceans, and third largest over most of the Atlantic Ocean.

Temperature changes have been small and variable in sign over the North Pacific Ocean, the Southern Ocean, and the regions of upwelling off the west coast of South America. p 11"

What are the specifics in the North Pacific Oceans and the Southern Ocean? Is it meant that GHG is not mixed all around the world equally?

Do you remember the following statement: *"(Charles David) Keeling (built the gas chromatograph)... and using his Mauna Loa measurements show that with each passing years CO2 levels were steadily moving upward"*?

"SUMMARY DISCUSSION

Human-made climate change has become an issue of surpassing importance to humanity [Hansen, 2009], and global warming is the first-order manifestation of increasing greenhouse gases that are predicted to drive climate change. Thus, it is understandable that analysis of ongoing global temperature change are now subject to increasing scrutiny and criticisms that are different than would occur f or a purely scientific problem."

Scrutiny must be applied to both the data of ongoing temperature change and MOSTLY to suggestions that *"increasing greenhouse gases that are predicted to drive climate change."* Data could be right, but if we have other reasons for climate change besides GHG, no one level of precision for this data could provide good policy directions.

"Our comments here about communication of this climate change science to the public are our opinion. Other people may have quite different opinions. We offer our opinion because it seems inappropriate to ignore the vast range of claims appearing in the media and in hopes that open discussion of these matters may help people distinguish the reality of global change sooner than would otherwise be the case. However, these comments, even though based on experience over a few decades, are only opinion."

If it is only opinion, my opinion that the properties of water are playing a bigger role than GHG in nature must be on the same level of attention. Where is *"that open discussion"*? If this is opinion, why can't I publish my point of view, my opinion in the media? Their opinion looks like an order to stop debate because of the *"reality of global change."* Yes, my opinion (I hope readers understand that it is the opinion of scientists like Gianniny, Chris Reij) is against the opinion of 98% of scientists. Even though it is different, it must be published on 50/50 level to the opinions of those 98%. We must be equal, and people in the world must have the opportunity to weigh ideas and make decisions. We have two opinions and only an equal discussion could choose the right direction for policy. Even after choosing one of them, we must always remember about the other opinion(s). Unfortunately, in the science of climate change, the majority wins. It is the main problem today with the science of climate change. The opinions of scientists like Gianniny and Chris Reij will always be suppressed by the wisdom of the majority.

"Communication of the status of global warming to the public has always been hampered by weather variability. Other obstacles to public communication include the media's difficulty in framing long-term problems as 'news,' a preference for sensationalism, a generally low level of familiarity with basic science, and a preference for 'balance' in every story. The difficulties are compounded by the politicization of reporting of global warming, a perhaps inevitable consequence of economic and social implications of efforts required to alter the course of human-made climate change. p 23.

It is very strange to read from a scientist's point of view that the *"preference for 'balance' in every story"* looks like sarcasm. We need that balance, which will push readers to think, and not to believe. In science, any new idea must be welcome, otherwise it will be stagnant science, as it is right now. The political slogan "Debate is over" became a reality check for this science in opposite direction, which scientists mean. It shows *'a generally low level of familiarity with basic science'* by a majority of scientists of climate change. Their recommendation to reduce the effect of climate change will bring to mankind more economical damage than WWI and WWII did together. They provide governments in the world with wrong and very expensive tools on how to fight climate change.

Let analyze article of Monte Hieb, Last updated: March 21, 2009, Climate and the Carboniferous Period, http://www.geocraft.com/WVFossils/Carboniferous_climate.html

*"Average global temperatures in the **EarlyCarboniferous Period** were **hot**- approximately **20° C (68° F)**. However, cooling during the Middle Carboniferous reduced average global temperatures to about **12° C (54° F)**... this is comparable to the average global temperature on Earth today!*

*Similarly, atmospheric concentrations of **carbon dioxide** (CO2) in the **Early Carboniferous Period** were approximately **1500 ppm** (parts per million), but by the **Middle Carboniferous** had declined to about **350 ppm**-- comparable to average CO2 concentrations today!"*

If we know, that the Carboniferous Period lasted from about 359.2 to 299 million years ago, it means that position of all continents was completely different than right now. Reasons for cooling in that period could depend on changing position of continent and many other reasons. In colder water will be always more carbon dioxide and other gases. Than more carbon dioxide in oceans, than less it in air.

*"Earth's atmosphere today contains about 380 ppm CO2 (0.038%). Compared to former geologic times, our **present** atmosphere, like the **Late Carboniferous** atmosphere, is**CO2 -impoverished!** In the last 600 million years of Earth's history only the **Carboniferous Period** and our present age, the **Quaternary Period,** have witnessed CO2 levels less than **400 ppm**.*

*There has historically been much more CO2 in our atmosphere than exists today. For example, during the **Jurassic Period** (200 mya), average CO2 concentrations were about **1800 ppm** or about 4.7 times higher than today. The highest concentrations of CO2 during all of the Paleozoic Era occurred during the **Cambrian Period**, nearly **7000 ppm**-- about 18 times higher than today.*

*The **Carboniferous Period** and the **Ordovician Period** were the only geological periods during the Paleozoic Era when **globaltemperatures were as low as they are today**. To the consternation of global warming proponents, the Late Ordovician Period was also an **Ice Age** while at the same time CO2 concentrations then were nearly 12 times higher than today-- **4400 ppm**. According to greenhouse theory, Earth should have been exceedingly hot. Instead, global temperatures were no warmer than today. Clearly, other factors besides atmospheric carbon influence Earth temperatures and global warming."*

Please pay attention to the following:

*"To the consternation of global warming proponents, the Late Ordovician Period was also an **Ice Age** while at the same time CO2 concentrations then were nearly 12 times higher than today-- **4400 ppm**. According to greenhouse theory, Earth should have been exceedingly hot. Instead, global temperatures were no warmer than today. Clearly, other factors besides atmospheric carbon influence Earth temperatures and global warming."*

If I found this information, scientists of climate change also must know it. Maybe they respond to it somewhere but I am sorry that in this case I did not found these responses.

Let look at article:

James Hansen, Makiko Sato, Pushker Kharecha, Gary Russel, David W. Lea and Mark Sidall, 2007 *Climate change and trace gases, http://rsta.royalsocietypublishing.org/content/365/1856/1925.full.pdf*

> *"Palaeoclimate data show that the Earth's climate is remarkably sensitive to global forcings. Positive feedbacks predominate. This allows the entire planet to be whipsawed between climate states. One feedback, the 'albedo flip' property of ice/water, provides a powerful trigger mechanism. A climate forcing that 'flips' the albedo of a sufficient portion of an ice sheet can spark a cataclysm. Inertia of ice sheet and ocean provides only moderate delay to ice sheet disintegration and a burst of added global warming. Recent greenhouse gas (GHG) emissions place the Earth perilously close to dramatic climate change that could run out of our control, with great dangers for humans and other creatures. Carbon dioxide (CO2) is the largest human-made climate forcing, but other trace constituents are also important. Only intense simultaneous efforts to slow CO2 emissions and reduce non-CO2 forcings can keep climate within or near the range of the past million years. p 1925*

Again and again, scientists of climate change are blaming carbon dioxide without any reasoning. Why are they doing so?

> *Records of climate change over the past several hundred thousand years carry a rich bounty of information about climate sensitivity. Here we use Antarctic temperature data of Vimeux et al. (2002) derived from an ice core extracted near Vostok (Petit et al. 1999), approximately 1000 km from the South Pole. Although a longer Antarctic record has been obtained (EPICA 2004), the Vimeux et al. (2002) temperatures are corrected for climate variation in the water vapour source regions and the record length is sufficient to match the sea level data of Siddall et al. (2003).*

Please pay attention that *"temperatures are corrected for climate variation in the water vapour source regions."* Scientists, a priori, take one of the properties of water-water vapor as GHG to make the statement that temperatures are corrected for climate variation *"in the water vapour source regions.'* If ALL properties of water are actually cooling the atmosphere, what does it mean for their correction?

"The Holocene is the current warm ('interglacial') period, now almost 12 000 years in duration. This climate record reveals repeated irregular cooling over periods of ca 100 000 years, terminated by rapid warmings of approximately 10ºC in Antarctica.

The largest temperature swings occurred almost synchronously throughout the planet. The amplitude of these temperature swings is typically 3–4ºC in tropical ocean regions (as revealed by the Mg/Ca composition of microscopic creatures that lived near the ocean surface, whose shells are preserved in ocean sediments; Lea et al. 2000), approximately 5ºC on global average and 10ºC near the poles.

The same Vostok ice core that defines past Antarctic temperature also reveals

the history of long-lived atmospheric gases. Bubbles of air are trapped as annual snowfalls pile up and compress gradually into ice. The Vostok records (Petit et al. 1999) of the two principal greenhouse gases (GHGs), CO_2 and CH_4 (methane), have been shown many times and are not repeated here. The record of the third major long-lived GHG, N_2O, is not preserved as well owing to reactions with organic matter in dust particles that are also trapped in the ice. However, the amplitude of the glacial–interglacial N_2O change is established from instances when dust amount was small (Spahni et al. 2005). Since the N_2O climate forcing is a small fraction of the total GHG forcing, and because time N_2O variations, where available, are similar to those of CO_2 and CH_4, it is possible to reconstruct accurately the climate forcing caused by the sum of all three long-lived GHGs. pages1926-1927

According to the opinion of scientists, all GHG-CO2, CH4, H2 O become a source of forcing climate, despite that we can't compare almost static positions of these gases in air with dynamic, which only properties of water bring to them. How is this dynamic picture omitted? Why did Hansen forget the cooling effect of vegetation and irrigation? Why did he forget that *"black carbon heats the air, increases convection and precipitation, and leads to larger surface cooling than if the aerosols were sulfates"*? It is impossible to imagine that scientist forget about the molecular weight of these gases. The molecular weight for CO2 is 44, for Oxygen-O2, it is 32; for Nitrogen-N2, it is 28; for CH4, it is 16; for H2 O, it is 18. Does it have no meaning for scientists of climate change? Which gases from them are lighter? Let suggest that we have two parcel of air. In one parcel it will be greenhouse gases like CO2 and N2 O and in another parcel greenhouse gases like CH4 and H2 O in equal concentration. Question is "will the influence of these gases in both parcels the same in abilities of these parcels to go UP or DOWN, especially if concentration of CH4 and H2 O could be in reality many times bigger than CO2 and N2O?Yes, all of them will trap infrared radiation of different bands, but only CH4, H2 O will help convection forces to bring a parcel of air UP, because these gases are lighter than CO2 and N2 O. Only water vapor has possibilities to recreate convection forces. If scientists did not see the differences in properties of different GHG, how is it that *"it is possible to reconstruct accurately the climate forcing caused by the sum of all three long lived GHGs"*?

Tyndall was not responsible for the wrong opinion of today's scientists of climate change.

If *"N2 O, is not preserved as well owing to reactions with organic matter in dust particles that are also trapped in the ice,"* why couldn't this dust be a huge forcing factor by decreasing reflection back to space of direct sun radiation?

> *"A word of explanation about climate forcings is needed. A forcing is an imposed change of the planet's energy balance with space. The most common technical measure of forcing (Hansen et al. 1997;*

IPCC 2001) is the adjusted forcing (Fa). Fa is the imbalance, caused by the forcing agent, between solar energy absorbed by the planet and thermal emission to space, measured after stratospheric temperature adjusts to presence of the agent. However, it is useful to account for the fact that some forcing agents have greater 'efficacy' than others for changing global temperature, especially when indirect effects of the forcing agent are included (Hansen et al. 2005a). Thus, CH4 has efficacy of approximately 1.4, i.e. it causes 40% more temperature change than does a CO2 forcing of the same magnitude, primarily because increased CH4 causes an increase in tropospheric O3 and stratospheric H2 O. The factor 1.4 accounts for the efficacy of CH4 and the factor 1.15 accounts approximately for forcing by N2 O, as the glacial–interglacial N2O forcing is approximately 15% of the sum of CO2 and CH4 glacial–interglacial forcings (Hansen et al. 2005a; Spahni et al. 2005)"

Maybe "*CH4 causes an increase in tropospheric O3 and stratospheric H2 O,*".Question is how scientists could forget that both gases as methane, as water vapor are lighter than most gases in the air? Because of that fact, they bring dynamic properties to all gases in the air, moving them UP to the upper troposphere. It must be researched, what will prevails in their behavior is that the cooling air by helping to move all gases to the upper troposphere and up, or heating effect, is because they are GHG and trapped IR radiation. Scientists of the climate change are always looking at GHG only as these gases have only one property-trap infrared radiation and heat the air. If CH4 increases stratospheric water vapor, is it so difficult to suggest that the condensation of water vapor in an ice crystal will release its energy which will go to space more easily than from ground level? Or maybe methane, as a lighter gas, will not be involved in the movement UP of all other gases? Could carbon dioxide have the same influence on a parcel of air? It is ridiculous that scientists, who study climate change all their lives, did not see these simple discrepancies in their studies. It is a shame for the peer review process to omit these discrepancies.

"...remarkable correspondence of Vostok temperature and global GHG climate forcing. The temperature change appears to usually lead the gas changes by typically several hundred years, as discussed below...

This suggests that warming climate causes a net release of these GHGs by the ocean, soils and biosphere. GHGs are thus a powerful amplifier of climate change, comparable to the surface albedo feedback, as quantified below."

Warming climate released GHG—it is understandable, but to claim that these gases are a powerful amplifier of climate change, we need to believe in special powers of GHG. In this case, it is not a science but rather a religious dogma from the mistake of Arrhenius.

Tyndall did nothing to support this mistake.

For some reason, today's science of climate change is going in Arrhenius's direction and involves the authority of Tyndall to make its case. If we make bonfire in a wigwam, almost all heat will stay there because the movement of air inside is restricted by a small hole on top of the wigwam. A bonfire outside will move all heat energy UP. This is the difference between the vision of climate change by 98% of scientists and reality.

Water vapor and other properties of water and methane are the main sources of moving "hot" air from the surface of the Earth UP to cloud level. It is so obvious and so strange that 98% of scientists are so blind in their love of GHG.

"The GHGs, because they change almost simultaneously with the climate, are a major 'cause' of glacial-to-interglacial climate change,... even if, as seems likely, they slightly lag the climate change and thus are not the initial instigator of change."

What is *"the initial instigator of change"*? Why do we need to blame GHG for climate change? If *"they slightly lag the climate change,"* why do we need to believe that they are responsible for any changes in climate? If scientists haven't any knowledge of other reasons, why do we need to believe that GHG are these reasons?

Do we need forgive scientists and make them lucky for their lack of imagination?

"The temperature–GHG lag is imprecise because the time required for snow to pile high enough (approx. 100 m) to seal off air bubbles is typically a few thousand years in central Antarctica..."

Let's suggest that a few thousand years is 2,000 years. For these 2,000 years, snow piles will be approximately 100 m. This means that every year there will be an accumulation of 5 cm of snow, of course it will be under pressure and close by density to ice. Let's remember that.

"Despite multiple careful studies, uncertainties in the ice–gas age differences for the Vostok ice core remain of the order of 1 kyr (Bender et al. 2006). Therefore, we can only say with certainty that the temperature and gas changes are nearly synchronous."

We have uncertainties of the order of 1,000 years and at the same time, *"we can only say with certainty that the temperature and gas changes are nearly synchronous."* During one thousand of years ice will be melted. Imagine how much black carbon, dusts from volcano activities, and thunderstorms will be uncovered on the surface of ice. I am sure that the surface of ice, even if it will not be wet, will be black as coal with almost zero reflection of direct sun radiation. Will this blackness of ice not take almost 100% of direct sun radiation? If so, why do we need to involve GHG in the explanation of the fast-occurring process of warming in the history of the Earth?

"Data from a different Antarctic (Dome C) ice core with slightly higher snow accumulation rate (Monnin et al. 2001) and an independent analysis based on argon isotopes (Caillon et al. 2003) support temperature leading GHGs by 600–800 years. In addition, carbon cycle models yield increases of GHGs in response to warming oceans and receding ice sheets.

Ice cores from Maud Land (EPICA 2006), which has very high snow deposition rates, should establish leads and lags accurately, but the present paper has only slight dependence on that result"

Please pay attention that these scientists admit that *"temperature leading GHGs by600–800 years."* Why did they do that?

Oh, it is so simple: *"This suggests that warming climate causes a net release of these GHGs by the ocean, soils and biosphere. GHGs are thus a powerful amplifier of climate change, comparable to the surface albedo feedback, as quantified below."* Higher temperatures of water in oceans released CO_2 into the atmosphere. It was the result of Global Warming, no reasons for it. Obsession with GHG theory again brings scientists of climate change to speculate that the releasing of GHG by oceans is acting as a forcing factor. Only peer reviewed censorship could explain that thousands of scientists can't see the discrepancy in GHG theory. There is something deeply wrong with the science of climate change. Instead of an explanation of possible reasons, they used speculations about GHG theory, which is full of discrepancies.

"Ice sheet and Sea-Level Change

Earth's energy balance is affected by changes on the planetary surface, as well as in the atmosphere. The important surface change is the albedo (reflectivity) for solar radiation. Surface albedo changes as areas of ice, vegetation and exposed l and change" pages 1928,1929

We need to take from Wikipedia that *"for the past millions years this was occurred over and over again at 100,000 year intervals. About 80-90,000 years of ice age with about 10-20,000 years of warm period... It is mainly due to Milankovitch cycles."* Please Google "Milankovitch cycles" to better understand the influence of the Sun on the climate of the Earth.

Authors are trying to explain why warming is so fast, while cooling is significantly longer. What kind of changes do they see on the planetary surface? They are talking about the reflectivity for direct sun radiation. Please do not forget that even in a warming period, warming occurs in a few thousands of years.

"Surface albedo changes as areas of ice, vegetation and exposed land change."

Authors supposed that ice reflects to space more direct sun radiation than vegetation and exposed land. I invite readers to place where during the winter a city authority gathers all the snow from the street. It is usually a mount of snow more than 10 m high. In a snowing winter, it is usually white by color. In the springtime, this mount becomes very black and dirty quickly. Why is that?

This "mount of snow" accumulates black carbon, dust, and other dirty things during the wintertime and, very quickly, as a thin cover of fresh snow is melting, this dirty part of snow mount becomes dirtier as soon as every additional layer of snow is melted.

It wasn't mankind's influence on the ice at that time; it was the eruption of the volcanos and thunderstorms in area close to Equator, and many other sources of dust, which covered the surface of ice every year. In a cooling period of around 80,000 years, it will bring a lot of "dirty" things onto the surface of any ice in any period of Earth's history. Only in a cooling period in the summertime will new snow cover these "dirty" things very quickly and reflectivity is high.

I WANT TO UNDERLINE THAT IN A WARMING PERIOD, THE MELTING OF LAYERS OF ICE ACCUMULATED DURING FIVE–TEN YEARS WILL MAKE THE SURFACE OF ICE THE SAME AS WE SEE IN OUR LIFE ON THE "MOUNT OF SNOW" COLLECTED DURING THE THREE MONTHS OF WINTER AFTER THE FIRST MELTING IN SPRINGTIME.

After the melting of ice during the first five–ten years, the surface of all ice which covers the Earth will be black as coal and will take almost 100% of sun radiation. This is more likely the real reason for the fast warming effect during the warming period of Milankovitch cycles.

"Fast feedbacks include changes of water vapour, clouds, climate-driven aerosols, sea ice and snow cover. This empirical result for the 'Charney'

climate sensitivity agrees well with that obtained by climate models (IPCC 2001).

However, the empirical 'error bar' is smaller and, unlike the model result, the empirical climate sensitivity certainly incorporates all processes operating in the real world." p 1929

If we will take in consideration "black surface of ice" after few years of melting, changes in water vapor, clouds, climate driven aerosols are laughable reasons for explanation of fast warming of Earth in that period.

> *"The empirical climate sensitivity based on the last ice age can be tested for longer periods using sea-level data... The impact of differences among the three records on results... is readily envisaged, as effects are linear. We cannot rely on timing of sea-level changes to better than several thousand years because it includes 'orbital tuning', i.e. slight time-scale adjustments to make major features line up with Earth's orbital changes. Thus, although relative timing of GHG and Antarctic temperatures, from the same ice core, are good within ca 1000 years or less, dating inconsistency of sea-level change with respect to these other two quantities is as much as several thousand years. Temporal resolution in the sea-level data is also coarser than in the ice core data."*

Scientists honestly admit that the *"temporal resolution in the sea-level data is also coarser than in the ice core data."* Is it a big deal between one thousand years and several thousand years? Sorry, that I am very sarcastic man, when I read articles of climate scientists.

" Sea-level change yields an estimate of ice sheet area change. As ice sheets grow they become thicker, as well as larger in both horizontal dimensions. Thus, we take ice sheet horizontal area as proportional to the two-third power of the amount of water locked in the ice sheets."

It is a mistake to think that *"as ice sheets grow they become thicker, as well as larger in both horizontal dimensions."* It can't be equal in all dimensions in all places. In colder areas, such as on mounts and close to the poles, ice grows vertically better than horizontally.

In this case, the horizontal area will never be proportional to the amount of water locked in the ice sheets.

Let's look at the Greenland ice sheet according to Wikipedia (Encyclopedia Britannica. 1999, Multimedia edition:

*"The Greenland ice sheet (*__Kalaallisut__*: Sermersuaq) is a vast body of* __ice__ *covering 1,710,000 square kilometres (660,235 sq mi), roughly 80% of the surface of* __Greenland__*. It is the second largest ice body in the world... The ice sheet is almost 2,400 kilometres (1,500 mi) long in a north-south direction, and its greatest width is 1,100 kilometres (680 mi) at a latitude of* __77°N__*, near its northern margin. The mean altitude of the ice is 2,135 metres (7,005 ft.) ().*

The thickness is generally more than 2 km (1.24 mi) ... and over 3 km (1.86 mi) at its thickest point."

You see, the differences in thickness of ice sheet could be more than 1 km.

> *"It is not the only ice mass of Greenland—isolated* __glaciers__ *and small* __ice caps__ *cover between 76,000 and 100,000 square kilometres (29,344 and 38,610 sq mi) around the periphery. Some scientists predict that* __climate change__ *may be about to push the ice sheet over a threshold where the entire ice sheet will melt in less than a few hundred years. If the entire 2,850,000 cubic kilometres (683,751 cu mi) of ice were to melt, it would lead to a global* __sea level rise__ *of 7.2 m (23.6 ft) (Climate Change 2001: The Scientific Basis. Contribution of Working Group I to the Third Assessment Report of the Intergovernmental Panel on Climate Change (IPCC) [Houghton, J.T.,Y. Ding, D.J. Griggs, M. Noguer, P.J. van der Linden, X. Dai, K. Maskell, and C.A. Johnson (eds.)]. Cambridge University Press, Cambridge, United Kingdom and New York, NY, USA, 881pp.*

If the melting of Greenland ice will raise the sea level by 7.2 m, it is correct to suggest that, under cooling conditions, only Greenland's ice sheet will take back the same 7.2 m of sea level and no one square cm of horizontal two dimensions will be added for changing the albedo of Greenland. If the thickness of ice is more than 2 km and over 3 km *"at its thickest point,"* why do we need to suggest that in Greenland *"as ice sheets grow they become thicker, as well as larger in both horizontal dimensions."* Is Greenland such a unique place on the Earth? What about Antarctica and its ice sheets? We could find thousands of places on the Earth where ice grows mostly UP rather than horizontal. It is ridiculous that peer reviewed scientists do not see these discrepancies. I can't understand why it is happening.

Let return back to article: James Hansen, Makiko Sato, Pushker Kharecha, Gary Russel, David W. Lea and Mark Sidall, 2007 Climate change and trace gases

"Normalization of surface albedo forcing is 3.5Wm² (equivalent to approximately 1.5% reduction of solar irradiance, as the Earth absorbs approximately 240Wm² of solar energy) at the time of the last ice age, when sea level was approximately 110 m lower than today.

"Albedo effects due to continental shelf exposure and vegetation migration are included within this empirical evaluation..."

If this empirical evaluation is on the same level as suggestions about both horizontal dimensions for ice sheets, albedo evaluations can't be reliable.

"When the surface albedo and GHG forcings ...are added and multiplied by the climate sensitivity ... the calculated temperature... is obtained. This calculated temperature is compared to the Vostok temperature change divided by 2, which we take as an approximation of global temperature change. The remarkable coincidence of calculated and observed temperatures cannot be accidental. The close agreement has dramatic implications for interpretation of past climate change and for expectation of future climate change due to human-made climate forcings."

Examples of Greenland show nothing remarkable in calculated and observed temperatures. It is an absolutely questionable result and coincidence in this case only shows systematical mistakes in suggestions by involved scientists and the peer reviewed herd.

"We include climate-driven aerosol changes and their cloud effects as a 'fast feedback' because aerosols respond rapidly to climate change.

This choice yields a more precise empirical climate sensitivity because aerosol forcing depends sensitively on uncertain aerosol absorption. Our inferred climate sensitivity, 3ºC for doubled CO2 , is the same as estimated by Hansen et al. (1993), who did not classify aerosols as a fast feedback, because our present omission of the small net aerosol forcing is compensated by larger effective GHG forcings, especially the high efficacy (140%) of CH4 . Ice core data show that aerosols decrease as the climate warms, probably because increased water vapour and rainfall wash out aerosols. Aerosol amount in the Earth's atmosphere seems to have decreased in the past two decades (Mishchenko et al. 2007), while human-made aerosol sources were believed to be increasing. We suggest that the aerosol decrease may be due to rapid global warming, approximately 0.2ºC per decade (Hansen et al. 2006a), and resulting moistening of the atmosphere"
P 1929

It is a very good example how many smart thoughts and suggestions scientists must provide, how much data is input for their calculations to make scientifically good-looking absurdity without any touch of reality. Please read this scientific joke:

"We include climate-driven aerosol changes and their cloud effects as a 'fast feedback' because aerosols respond rapidly to climate change. This choice yields a more precise empirical climate sensitivity because aerosol forcing depends sensitively on uncertain aerosol absorption."

Unfortunately, they are not joking. Dirty ice surface is taking sun radiation. Dirty garbage data putting into computers produces garbage, which is a shame for today's science of climate change.

"Causes of palaeoclimate fluctuations... with surface albedo and long-lived GHG amounts specified, the magnitude of Pleistocene climate variations is accounted for by fast feedback processes (climate-driven changes of water vapour, aerosols, clouds, sea ice and snow). However, implications of the large palaeoclimate swings... reach far beyond confirmation that the Charney (fast feedback) climate sensitivity is approximately 3ºC for doubled CO2." p 1930

Scientists have even found that "climate sensitivity is approximately 3ºC for doubled CO2." They substitute a more likely real reason—"blackness" of ice by increasing the amount of GHG in the atmosphere and assuring people how smart their computer models are. They do not even try to find another explanation. As good soldiers, they are forcing in one direction. Sorry soldiers, I don't want to insult you. There are thousands of scientists and only one direction. If the direction is wrong, it is wrong, even if a million scientists support this direction. Is it so remarkable, or so wrong? What is probably good for an army is always wrong for science.

> "Antarctic temperature change divided by 2 serves as a crude 'global thermometer' for large global climate change on time-scales of several thousand years or longer. Limitations of a local thermometer are obvious on time-scales of 1–2 kyr or less, when Antarctic and Greenland temperature fluctuations are often on a 'see-saw', i.e. out of phase (EPICA 2006). Leads and lags of temperature changes at different locations are crucial for understanding the mechanisms of climate change, and these short-term variations can involve complex dynamical processes, including possible 'reorganizations' of ocean and atmospheric circulation. However, global temperature changes must be coherent in the two hemispheres for any climate forcings large enough to change tropical ocean temperature, because the tropics, via ocean and atmosphere, export heat to both hemispheres. Indeed, a coherent global response occurs even for forcings predominately located in one hemisphere, such as anthropogenic aerosols or change of ice sheet area, although the response is larger in the hemisphere with greater forcing (Hansen et al. 2005a)" p. 1930.

This is a very important moment: "Leads and lags of temperature changes at different locations are crucial for understanding the mechanisms of climate change, and these short-term variations can involve complex dynamical processes, including possible 'reorganizations' of ocean and atmospheric circulation."

"Possible reorganizations of ocean and atmospheric circulation" could be in our time. These reorganizations could be under human control and help fight climate change, if we correctly understand the real reasons, which influence climate. These real reasons can't be estimated by a percentage of supported scientists of climate change.

> *"The last glacial cycle, the most accurately dated, has two notable discrepancies between observed and calculated temperature. The first calculation discrepancy is failure to obtain a deep minimum temperature at Marine Isotope Stage (MIS)... (ca 110 kyr BP)...*

> *The second discrepancy occurs in the last 8000 years, with calculated temperature rising rapidly while observed temperature fell. Calculated warming is due to increase of CO2 from approximately 260 to 275 ppm and CH4 from approximately 600 to 675 ppb. Ruddiman (2003) suggests that the GHG increases are due to deforestation beginning ca 8 kyr BP and rice agriculture beginning ca 5 kyr BP. Indeed, much of the observed GHG increase is plausibly anthropogenic, but we would expect early negative anthropogenic forcings from the same agricultural and deforestation activities, due to aerosols and surface albedo change,... to exceed positive GHG forcings. The aerosol forcing, especially indirect effects on clouds, is strongly nonlinear, with human-made aerosols in a nearly pristine atmosphere being much more effective than those added to the present atmosphere. Thus, although Ruddiman's basic thesis is probably correct, his conclusion that humans saved the Earth from an ice age is probably not right" p 1930*

It will be interesting to read an explanation of WHY *"human-made aerosols in a nearly pristine atmosphere being much more effective than those added to the present atmosphere."* These discrepancies occur only because scientists put into their computer models the wrong suggestions that GHG are the main players in nature. The same as the fact that they ignore the "blackness" of melted ice cover on the Earth and put the increasing of GHG as the main sources of warming. In our time they forget about the changes in the cooling effect of forests, which is significantly bigger than the cooling effect of any fields.

Deforestation, tilling of land for crop production, created reason for climate change, but these and other real reason is difficult or impossible to put in computer. The simplicity of blaming

GHG, which is supported by naming Tyndall and Arrhenius, and the success of results in computation brings hundreds, if not thousands, of scientists into the circle of 98% of snobs, which do not even look at other scientists' opinion. Tyndall will never be proud that his name is used to support GHG theories. This is the real irony and tragedy of our days. Their mistakes create billions of supporters in the world, which can't understand that scientists could make mistakes. While scientists are writing the results of their work in scientific journals, famous politicians like Al Gore, Bill Clinton, Tony Blair, Ban Ki Moon, Barack Obama, and many, many others have created a club of policymakers—supporters of solar cells, windmills, nuclear power plants, ethanol production, all of which are disastrous for our economy and environment."*Surface albedo and GHG amounts are themselves feedbacks that respond to climate change, implying that actual climate sensitivity is much greater than that due to fast feedbacks.*"

Surface albedo is real feedback, but estimation on how it works was wrong if we look at Greenland and Antarctica, as well as many other places where large amounts of ice could grow without any changes in the areas of ice sheets.

"Realization that climate sensitivity is larger on longer time-scales is not new, but larger sensitivities are usually thought to apply to millennial time-scales. We will argue that 'slow' feedbacks (ice sheet, vegetation and GHG) substantially influence century, and perhaps shorter time-scales."

We must change our definition of "slow" feedbacks to ice sheets, vegetation, and greenhouse gases. If we suggest that melting ice sheets uncover all black particles from a volcano's eruption, dust from thunderstorms, etc, the reduction of reflection of direct sun radiation will be changed very fast; it will warm the Earth very fast and can't be mentioned as slow feedback. Vegetation and GHG influence could be the opposite of what these authors think.

"We will argue that 'slow' feedbacks (ice sheet, vegetation and GHG) substantially influence century, and perhaps shorter time-scales.

Empirical analysis depends upon accurate knowledge of time-dependent forcings. One forcing mechanism is well known (Berger

1978): changes in the seasonal distribution of solar radiation impinging on the planet due to slow Earth's orbital changes (inclination of the spin axis, eccentricity of the orbit and season of closest approach to the Sun, i.e. precession of the equinoxes). The global mean forcing due to orbital variations is small: with a fixed surface albedo distribution, the maximum global mean forcing due to orbital variations is approximately 0.25W/m²."

Let's look at what it means for the forcing of 0.25W/m². In one year = 31,556,926 seconds. It means that during one year on every square meter of Earth's surface will come additional energy equal to:

$$0.25W/m^2 \text{ X } 31,556,926 \text{ sec X } 1 \text{ m}^2 = 7,889,231 \text{ J}$$

If we remember that 1Kcal = 4,184 J, we could calculate that 7,889,231J = 1885Kcal of energy. For ice latent heat of melting = 80Kcal/kg.

$$1885Kcal/80Kcal/kg = 23.5 \text{ kg}.$$

It means that with the additional forcing of 0.25W/m², we could melt during one year at every square meter of the Earth's surface 23.5 kg of ice. The density of ice is 917 kg/m³. Its means that 23.5 kg of ice has volume equal to 0.0255 m³ or it will be 25,500 cm³ of ice, which will be additionally melted during one year in an area of one square meter = 10,000 cm², or it will melt a layer of ice 2.5 cm per year. Summary of this calculations could provide that forcing factor of 0.25W/m² could melt as high as 2.5 cm of ice on every one square meter per year.

"This small forcing leaves an easily discernable impact on the spectrum of climate variability (Hays et al. 1976), even though a greater portion of variability has the character of red noise (Wunsch 2003). It appears that global climate is remarkably sensitive to even small forcings, and thus also to unforced climate fluctuations (chaos)."

If we understand the "blackness" of the surface of melted ice, we could easily understand that *"unforced climate fluctuations (chaos),"* perhaps wind, which collects in one place the dust from an eruption of a volcano, increasing melting in that area and uncover additional areas of "blackness" of ice in the closest places.

"Timing of insolation changes is known with great precision. Unfortunately, dating of past climate change is often influenced by orbital data (orbital tuning) using preconceived ideas about orbital effects on climate...

Analysis must begin with the predominant feature, the asymmetry of the ice ages, defined by global warmings that terminated the major ice ages. The warmings at ca 15, 130, 240 and 330 kyr BP are named Terminations I, II, III and IV, respectively. Such huge rapid climate change had to involve large positive feedbacks. Indeed... those feedbacks were surface albedo and GHGs. What we want to know is how those feedbacks worked."

If the scientists who analyze climate change do not understand that the growth of ice is not equal in horizontal and vertical dimensions and occurs mostly UP in the form of a cone their analysis can't be trusted. Layers of dust and black carbon will be opened faster and create positive feedback of "blackness" differently on different sides of these cones, depending on the angle, for incoming sun radiation. It is also true for hills and mounts areas.

"Note first that 'minor' mismatches in timing of observed and calculated temperatures... are due to dating errors and, to a lesser degree, limitations of a local thermometer. Proof is obtained by considering the contrary: ice sheet forcing approximately $3 Wm^2$ and a 5 kyr timing gap between forcing and response, as appears to be the case at Termination IV,... is $15\ 000 Wyr\ m^2$, enough to warm the upper kilometre of the ocean by approximately $160ºC$ ...

Obviously, no such warming occurred, nor did warming more than approximately 1/100th of that amount."

Here authors could analyze reasons for why warming wasn't so big. In this case, they must, of course, involve the cooling effect of evaporation, condensation, and other properties of water. It can't be that scientists do not know these properties of water, but their attentions are mostly concentrated on albedo from ice and wet ice, and effects of greenhouse gases in their interpretation.

"Forcing and temperature change had to be synchronous within a few centuries, at most, for the large global climate change at terminations.

Rapid warming at terminations, we assert, must be due to the fact that ice sheet disintegration is a wet process that, spurred by multiple thermodynamical and dynamical feedback processes (Hansen 2005), can proceed rapidly. Chief among these feedbacks is the large change in absorbed solar energy that occurs with the 'albedo flip' when snow and ice become wet. This process determines the season at which insolation anomalies are most important."

We have another example of speculation about *"the 'albedo flip' when snow and ice become wet."* It is correct right now when we are close to as dangerous of a situation as global warming. During springtime there is melting in some places of more than 3 meters of snow. Of course, this fast melting process will wet snow and ice and we could speak about *'albedo flip'* by wet snow and ice. In situation, when forcing is (so slow as) *0.25W/m²*, it is such a slow process that all the water from melted ice will be evaporated rather than wet ice and snow. We don't need to forget that we have *"a 5 kyr timing gap between forcing and response."* How black will the snow be during these 5 kyr? What will it mean for "wet ice" and "wet snow" in this case?

"Forcing and temperature change had to be synchronous within a few centuries, at most, for the large global climate change at terminations.

Rapid warming at terminations, we assert, must be due to the fact that ice sheet disintegration is a wet process that, spurred by multiple thermodynamical and dynamical feedback processes (Hansen 2005), can proceed rapidly. Chief among these feedbacks is the large change in absorbed solar energy that occurs with the 'albedo flip' when snow and ice become wet. This process determines the season at which insolation anomalies are most important."

A small forcing factor of 0.25W/m² could melt a layer of ice 2.5 cm per year. It is too slow process to make ice wet. Maybe it is better to think about the sublimation process rather than melting. Anyway, during a few centuries or 5 kyr, it will uncover step-by-step more particles of black carbon, dust, and other particles which create blackness on the surface of ice. There is no way that *"forcing and temperature change had to be synchronous within a few centuries, at most, for the large global climate change at terminations."* Forcing could be huge, but temperature will not change significantly until the time when most of the glacier area will be melted. There is no way that "albedo flip" could be explained by wet ice.

> *"The Milankovitch (1941) theory of the ice ages assumes that summer insolation* (incoming solar radiation) *anomalies at high latitudes in the Northern Hemisphere (NH) drive the ice ages:*
>
> *minimum summer insolation allows snow and ice accumulated in the cold season to survive, while maximum summer insolation tends to melt the ice sheets.*
>
> *We suggest, however, that spring is the critical season for terminations, because the albedo feedback works via the large change in absorbed sunlight that begins once the ice/snow surface becomes wet, after which the surface albedo remains low until thick fresh snow accumulates. A spring maximum of insolation anomaly pushes the first melt earlier in the year, without comparable shortening of autumn melt, thus abetting ice sheet disintegration. And an increase of GHGs stretches the melt season both earlier and later, while also increasing midsummer melt. Thus, it is not surprising that Terminations I, II, III and IV all had strong maxima in GHG forcing, as well as, we presume, favourable insolation. Pages 1931, 1932*

How strange is it to read about spring, summer, and autumn "melt" and "wet" from scientists who understand that we need at least a *"few centuries, at most, for the large global climate change at terminations"*? These discrepancies only underscore the reasons to reevaluate the science of climate change together with the entire peer review system in this science. It is easy to take from the same ice cores which scientists use—*"Here we use Antarctic temperature data of Vimeux et al. (2002) derived from an ice core extracted near*

Vostok (Petit et al. 1999)"—and other stations to find how much black carbon and other dust-collected ice even in places close to the poles for 0.01,0.05, 0.1, 0.2, 0.3, 0.4, 0.5, 1.0, 1.5, 2 kilo years.

I hope you remember: *"The important surface change is the albedo (reflectivity) for solar radiation."*

Scientists could melt ice collected for these 0.01, 0.05, 0.1, 0.2, 0.3, 0.4, 0.5, 1.0, 1.5, 2 kilo years and measure accordingly the reflectability of the mix of dust and black carbon as a result of this melting. If after that they would put into their computer models the results of the heating of the Earth by reduction of reflection of direct sun radiation, there would be no need for *"wet ice,"*or GHG effects, or other speculations in their models.

> *"Dangerous climate change.*
>
> *Emergence of human-caused global warming raises the question: what level of further warming will be 'dangerous' for humanity?*
>
> *...it may be useful in considering this issue to contrast today's climate with the warmest interglacial periods and with the middle Pliocene, when global temperature was 2–3ºC warmer than today.*
>
> *Antarctic temperature was a few degrees warmer in the warmest interglacial periods, but temperature there is magnified by high latitude feedbacks and dependent upon the altitude of the ice surface. The tropical Pacific and Indian Oceans are especially relevant: the Pacific is a driver of global climate, and the Indian Ocean has the highest correlation with global temperature in the period of instrumental data (Hansen et al. 2006a)...*
>
> *There is an uncertainty of approximately 1ºC in the calibration of palaeoproxy temperature with modern data. However, ocean surface temperature at the beginning of modern measurements (late nineteenth century) must have been within the Holocene temperature range, so the error... not exceed several tenths of a degree Celsius."*

We have *"an uncertainty of approximately 1ºC in the calibration of palaeoproxytemperature with modern data."* And at the same time the *"ocean surface temperature at the beginning of modern measurements (late nineteenth century) must have been within the Holocene temperature range, so the error... not exceed several tenths of a degree Celsius."*

Why must we assume that the*"ocean surface temperature at the beginning of modern measurements (late nineteenth century) must have been within the Holocene temperature range"*? Let me remind you that *"The* **Holocene...** *began around 12,000 years ago and continues to the present."*

How is it possible that *"an uncertainty of approximately 1ºC"* AND an *"error... not exceed several tenths of a degree Celsius"*? To understand what mean Proxy Data let look in educational article (without name of author):

Paleo Proxy Data, 2003 "www.ncdc.noaa.gov/paleo/proxies.htm

"Paleoclimatologists gather proxy data from natural recorders of climate `variability such as tree rings, ice cores, fossil pollen, ocean sediments, corals and historical data. By analyzing records taken from these and other proxy sources, scientists can extend our understanding of climate far beyond the 100+ year instrumental record."

Ocean surface temperature at the beginning of modern measurements *"must have been within the Holocene temperature range, so the error... not exceed several tenths of a degree Celsius."*

If proxy data for Holocene compared with today's modern measurements give errors, which do *"not exceed several tenths of a degree Celsius,"* why do we need all these instruments today? Or how could we use proxy measurements for a situation 12,000 years ago and give them today's level of errors by very precise tools, which we use for today's measurements?

"We conclude that the warming of the past several decades has brought today's temperature to or near the Holocene maximum and within approximately 1ºC of the warmest interglacial periods.

Sea level following Termination II may have reached 4±2 m higher than today (Overpeck et al. 2006), which would already qualify as dangerous change. It is possible, but uncertain, that such a sea-level rise would occur with additional warming less than 1ºC today."

Please pay attention: *"It is possible, but uncertain..."* It is also strange that proxy data for Holocene are giving *"error... not exceed several tenths of a degree Celsius,"* while in *"sea level following Termination II may have reached 4±2 m higher than today."*

Is it meant that *"several tenths of a degree Celsius,"* could provide uncertainty in sea level equal 4±2 m? Or maybe it means that proxy data for a period 12,000 years ago is so different from a period 140,000 years ago? Or is it a scientific joke for gullible readers?

Let's look at what Goddard Institute for Space Studies wrote about Pliocene.

> *"The Pliocene epoch covers the period from approximately 5 to 1.8 million years ago and, as such, spanned the period of time during which the Earth transitioned from relatively warm climates to the generally cooler climates of the Pleistocene. This transition included the emergence of the direct ancestors of humankind and contains the beginnings of cyclic Northern Hemisphere glaciation. The Pliocene epoch itself contains episodic climate fluctuations prior to the late Pliocene cooling, and our focus for study is a warm period in the middle Pliocene between 3.15 and 2.85 million years before present."*

The Earth *"transitioned from relatively warm climates to the generally cooler climates of the Pleistocene."* It also was the *"beginnings of cyclic Northern Hemisphere glaciation."* After that it will be very interesting to read how climate change scientists are trying to fool the population: *"But what is clear is that global warming to the level of the middle Pliocene, when sea level was 25±10 m higher, would be exceedingly dangerous."*

If Pliocene occurred 5 to 1.8 million years ago were all continents at that time on the same place on the Earth as right now? What was real reason for transition from relatively warm climates to the cooler climates of the Pleistocene?

(Pleistocene- Wikipedia, the free encyclopedia*en.wikipedia.org/wiki/***Pleistocene***:

*"The **Pleistocene** (symbol PS) is the geological epoch which lasted from about 2588000 to 11700 years ago,)"*

Why scientists are using sea level of warm period on the Earth as fear factor for today warming? It is a really good and very scientific remark for idiots. Is global warming of today's level the end of cyclic *"Northern Hemisphere glaciation"*? Is it a science or is it a scenario for the next movie?

"Global warming of approximately 3ºC is predicted by practically all climate models for 'business-as-usual' (BAU) growth of GHGs (IPCC 2001, 2007). Yet IPCC (2001, 2007) foresees twenty-first century sea-level rise of only a fraction of a metre with BAU global warming. Their analysis assumes an inertia for ice sheets that, we argue, is incompatible with palaeoclimate data and inconsistent with observations of current ice sheet behaviour."

Yes, it is business-as-usual. Speculation about GHG and wrong analysis will really move our civilization to sea level higher than 25 meters.

"BAU global warming (approx. 3ºC) would be magnified on the ice sheets, based on general high latitude amplifications found in palaeo records and in climate models, as well as local ice sheet warming due to albedo flip. As a result, large portions of West Antarctica and Greenland would be bathed in melt water.

Already areas of summer melt have increased rapidly on Greenland (Steffen et al. 2004), the melt season is beginning earlier and lasting longer, and summer melt is being observed on parts of West Antarctica."

Scientist must find real explanation for reason of melting ice on Greenland and Antarctica, before making any predictions. To stop these predictions we must reevaluate the science of climate change. These predictions will happen even if reduce the level of GHG back to 280 ppm. GHG are only indicators of human activities in wrong directions. We must change the directions of human activities and pay less attention to the amount of GHG in atmosphere. **Real problem is unusual transfer of heat from**

equator to poles, which in result will rise the sea level, GHG have nothing to do with this reality.

"There is little doubt that projected warmings under BAU would initiate albedo-flip changes as great as those that occurred at earlier times in the Earth's history. The West Antarctic ice sheet today is at least as vulnerable as any of the earlier ice sheets. The processes that give rise to nonlinear ice sheet response (almost universal retreat of ice shelves buttressing the West Antarctic ice sheet and portions of Greenland, increased surface melt and basal lubrication, speed-up of the flux of icebergs from ice streams to the ocean, ice sheet thinning and thus lowering of its surface in the critical coastal regions, and an increase in the number of 'icequakes' that signify lurching motions by portions of the ice sheets) are observed to be increasing..."

It is possible that these observations are correct and must be stopped. We have only one huge problem: these changes in nature have nothing to do with carbon dioxide and other GHG. Today, the science of climate change, by following mistakes of Arrhenius, are giving the wrong recommendations to governments in the world on how to save the planet from climate change.

"Despite these early warnings about likely future nonlinear rapid response, IPCC continues, at least implicitly, to assume a linear response to BAU forcings. Yet BAU forcings exceed by far any forcings in recent palaeoclimate history. Part of the explanation for the inconsistency between palaeoclimate data and IPCC projections lies in the fact that existing ice sheet models are missing realistic (if any) representation of the physics of ice streams and icequakes, processes that are needed to obtain realistic nonlinear behaviour. In the absence of realistic models, it is better to rely on information from the Earth's history. That history reveals large changes of sea level on century and shorter timescales.

All, or at least most, of glacial-to-interglacial sea-level rise is completed during the ca 6 kyr quarter cycle of increasing insolation forcing as additional portions of the ice sheet experience albedo flip. There is no evidence in the accurately dated terminations (I and II) of multi-millennia lag in ice sheet response. We infer that it would be not only dangerous, but also foolhardy to follow a BAU path for future GHG emissions. Pages 1935, 1936, 1937.It is a good comparison of today's climate with previous climates in Earth's history. In both cases, scientists blame GHG as the main reason for climate change. Their computer models provide results, which correlate with real pictures. These similarities could lead the imagination to stray from the direction of the real reason that is responsible in nature for climate change and blame only GHG. As a result, it will take the imaginations of scientists in the wrong direction on how to fight back against climate change. If we could overthrow this inertia of thinking, we could find the real reasons for climate change. In this case, we must look at carbon dioxide and other GHG in previous periods of Earth's history as only an indicator of the increasing and decreasing of temperatures. Afterall, it's mostly oceans that release more GHG during higher temperatures and take them back if the temperature decreases. In our days, the increasing of greenhouse gases by human activities also does not play a significant role in nature. Arguing with climate scientists, I am using their terminology-climate change, global warming, global cooling, despite I mention before that this terminology is fooling us and take our imagination from real problem-melting ice on continents, which will increase sea level. We must understand that if we will create condition for transport of energy from equator to poles melting of ice on continent could occur even in global cooling condition. Changes on continents by human activities create this kind of danger.

"Climate forcing scenarios

the IPCC BAU scenarios continue to be used as standard forcings for climate simulations, but there is no inherent reason that the world must follow BAU GHG growth rates..."

Of course, scientists recommend "very good tools" to reduce the amount of GHG in the air—reduction in using of fossil sources of energy in a time when the population is growing and their green directions like solar cells and windmills are working well only in the articles of actors like Redford, or columnists like Friedman.

"We also compare with the 'alternative' scenario of Hansen et al. (2000), which was defined with the objective of keeping added human-made climate forcing in the twenty-first century...

However, emissions of fossil fuel CO2 increased rapidly in the past decade, consistent with IPCC BAU and more rapid than the alternative scenario."

In this case, business-as-usual (BAU) is blaming GHG by IPCC and scientists of climate change. BAU is the reaction from supporters in mass media and politicians all around the globe.

Greenhouse gases are not guilty. Scientists, their gullible political supporters, and mass media hysteria who choose the wrong enemy to fight climate change, are guilty.

"If CO2 emissions continue to follow BAU for another decade, with annual emission increases averaging 2% per year, the emissions in 10 years will be 40% above those in the alternative scenario. In this case, it would be difficult, probably expensive and implausible, to get back on the path of the alternative scenario this half-century."

We do not need to reduce the amount of GHG in nature; we must change the direction of human activities to save the planet.

> *"Non- CO2 climate forcings are important, despite the fact that CO2 is the largest human-made climate forcing. Indeed, expected difficulties in slowing the growth rate of CO2 and eventually stabilizing atmospheric CO2 amount make the non- CO2 forcings all the more important. It now appears that only if reduction of the non- CO2 forcings is achieved, and CO2 growth is slowed, will it be possible to keep global temperature within or near the range of the warmest interglacial periods.*
>
> *Fortunately, observed growth paths of non- CO2 forcings exhibit promise.*
>
> *CH4 ...is increasing slower than even the alternative scenario, much slower than IPCC scenarios. This may be partly due to reduced losses from fossil fuels (reduced CH4 loss from leaky pipelines and*

venting at oil wells, and capture at coal mines), as well as efforts to capture CH4 at landfills and waste management facilities.

There is potential for greater reduction of CH4 emissions. Such reduction could also reduce tropospheric ozone (O3), an important GHG and a pollutant contributing to asthma and other respiratory diseases. The 'global warming potential' (GWP) assigned to CH4 in the Kyoto Protocol understates its effect on climate because it excludes indirect effects.

Growth of N2O is also falling below most scenarios, but only slightly. N2O is especially important owing to its long atmospheric lifetime, of the order of a century. There is substantial potential for reducing its growth rate, which is due in part to excessive use of nitrogen in fertilization practices. There are potential multiple benefits in reducing N2O emissions, but better understanding of nitrogen cycle is needed. It deserves greater attention and emphasis in climate mitigation efforts.

It would be better if all climate forcings were not packaged together and made interchangeable with CO2 in mitigation strategies. Sources of different gases are usually independent and greater progress is likely from complementary focused programmes. However, in regulations of a specific activity or industry, the rules should be based on information about the effect of the activity on all climate forcings." Pages 1937, 1938.

All of that sounds very scientific and because of that, it is ten times more dangerous for our future. These are scientific reasons for the most dangerous movements of our time—the green direction for our economy based on the obsession of scientists on GHG. Even if they mention properties of water, which cooling air in South China, or that vegetation and irrigation provided the cooling effect in some areas, they return to the main trumps in their thinking—GHG. So, this impossible inclination in so many scientists' minds could be compared with Aristotle's mistake about the Earth as the center of the solar system. For almost 2,000 years Aristotle's system of a mistake was dogma for very smart and educated people. It will be a tragedy for the human race if ideas that GHG are responsible for climate change exist for the next 10–20 years. The greatest paradox that these scientists of climate change make in their scientific articles – they are right, that we haven't enough time to be in the stage of Business As Usual (BAU). We haven't enough time to play Galileo games with today's science of climate change. It could confirm all adepts of this science. I will strongly advise everyone to read this article (James Hansen, Makiko Sato, Pushker Kharecha, Gary Russel, David W. Lea and Mark Sidall, 2007 Climate change and trace gases.)with 25 pages, 10 figures, and 4 pages with references. It is published in the prestigious scientific journal *Philosophical Transaction of the Royal Society A*. In this article, eighty-two references sources were peer reviewed. At the same time, in my opinion, all of them are scientifically sounded garbage, which overestimate the effect of GHG in nature. How could it be true for science in our days? My deepest apologies to readers for repeating almost the same statement a hundred times, but please look at newspapers, magazines, TV, and many other sources, which use the propaganda machine of today's science of climate change and calculate how many times they mention GHG during at least 30 years.

Water, Air, Forests, And Other Vegetation

(Note: Most of next data, which I use is from Wikipedia.)

"Approximately 505,000 cubic kilometers of water falls as precipitation each year; 398,000 cubic kilometers of it over the oceans. Globally averaged annual precipitation is 990 millimeters."

It will be interesting to calculate that over oceans we have 398,000/505,000=0.788 or 78.8% of all precipitation, despite that ocean area is only 71% of all area of the Earth.

PROPERTIES OF WATER

71% of the Earth is covered by water and 97% of it is in the oceans.

Cohesion – Water sticks to itself very easily. Adhesion – Water sticks very well to other things

Surface tension – Molecules on the surface are not surrounded by similar molecules on all sides and cohesion forces from inside the molecules create shapes for a small drop or plane surface (in glass).

$$1 Kcal = 4,186 J$$

Density of water: 1000 kg/m³, liquid (4ºC); 917 kg/m³, solid.

Melting point: 0ºC,

Molecular formula: H2O

Molar mass: 18.01528 g/mol

Boiling point: 99.98ºC

Latent heat of melting: 80Kcal/kg

Latent heat of evaporation: 539Kcal/kg

Specific heat, water: 1Kcal/kg ºC

Specific heat, ice: 0.5Kcal/kg ºC

Specific heat water vapor: 0.48Kcal/kg ºC

PROPERTIES OF AIR

One atmosphere (9100 kPa or 14.7 psi) is the amount of pressure that can lift water approximately 10.3 m.

A kilogram-force (kgf) is a gravitational metric unit of force. It is equal to the magnitude of the force exerted by one kilogram of mass in a 9.80665 m/s² gravitational field.

Weight of volume of water 10.3 m high with area of 1cm²:

1030 cm X 1cm² X 1 gf/cm³ = 1030 gf = 1.03 kgf.

One atmosphere = 1.03 kgf/cm²

Air density = 1.225 kg/m³

Specific heat = 0.24Kcal/kg ºC =1.005kJ/kg ºC

Globally averaged annual precipitation is 990 millimeters or 0.99 m.

If density of water is 1000 kg/m³, it is easy to calculate that on every square meter of the Earth's surface we have in average 990 kg of precipitation.

To evaporate this amount of water we need 539Kcal/kg x 990 kg=533,610Kcal.

If one atmosphere = 1.03kgf/cm², it means that the weight of all air above ocean level in an area of 1 cm² is 1.03kgf.

The weight of all air above ocean level in an area of 1 m² (100 cm x 100 cm=10,000 cm²) is 1.03kgf/cm² x 10,000 cm² = 10,300kgf. It means that the mass of this air will be 10,300 kg.

Air specific heat = 0.24Kcal/kg°C.

To heat 10,300 kg of air on 1°C we need 10,300 kg x 0.24Kcal/kg °C=2472Kcal/°C.

We know that on every square meter of the Earth's surface precipitation is 990 kg and we need 533,610Kcal to evaporate this amount of water.

At the same time, we know that all air above sea level on every square meter needs 2472Kcal to be heated on 1°C.

After that, it is easy to calculate that the energy needed to evaporate precipitation on every square meter could heat all the air above on 215.86°C:

533,610Kcal / 2472Kcal/°C = 215.86°C

Let's keep in mind that the energy needed to evaporate the annual amount of precipitation on every square meter could heat all the air above that square meter from sea level on 215.86°C.

We need energy to evaporate water. This energy cools the air close to the source of evaporation—surface of lakes, rivers, seas, oceans, wet land, grass, leaves of bushes, and trees. What will happen with water vapor? Because it's lighter than most gases in the air, it will make the closest parcel of air lighter and because of that, this parcel will go up. Heat from the sun also heats the land (water), which heats air. It creates convection forces, which are moving air up and it looks like water vapor helps convection forces to move the parcel of air up.

If you will look at smoke from a chimney, it is easy to see that the rising tail of smoke becomes almost horizontal very quickly. It is happening despite the temperature in an oven being more than 500ºC. The parcel of air with smoke, which makes the parcel visible, is cooled with height. If temperature of this parcel will be cooled the same as temperature of surrounding air it will be not any forces to move this parcel up. In this case we could say, that convection forces stop to work with height. Why, in this case, can we see water vapor, which became visible as water droplets, in clouds?

It is again one of the properties of water, condensation, which helps to keep the parcel of air going up. Condensation releases the same amount of energy as needed to evaporate water. This energy heats the parcel of air and keeps it moving up. Of course, we can't say that in reality we have the real parcel of air like in a balloon. In reality, it is always a dynamic process when part of the air is moving by wind and tears the real first parcel, which we start to analyze. The same wind evaporates part of the new water droplets, cools the air, and brings part of this new parcel down. Anyway, because of these realities, we have a dynamic movement of air up to cloud level. Even the tops of clouds are continuing to evaporate and bring water vapor to a higher level.

In "blue" sky, when we can't see clouds, it is important to understand that in air from the oceans, and land level, until the upper troposphere and higher, we always have water vapor and water droplets. These water droplets are constantly changing and stick to each other by cohesion and are divided, partially or completely, and evaporated by the energy of wind or radiation.

Cloud formations are the result of evaporation from oceans (land) level, as evaporation and condensation of water vapor from all levels of the atmosphere where we have water vapor. The sun heats the ground, energy from the ground heats the air, and the hotter the air the lighter it is and because it is lighter it going up (convection). Water vapor and droplets are parts of any parcel of air, which could hold less or more molecules and drops of water – together with energy released by condensation, which heat surrounding air are the biggest moving forces in mixing air all around atmosphere.

We could read about cloud in article:

Web Curator: P. Kay Costulis, 2002 Clouds,

http://asd-www.larc.nasa.gov/edu_act/clouds.html

*"**High-level clouds** High-level clouds form above 20,000 feet (6,000 meters) and since the temperatures are so cold at such high elevations, these clouds are primarily composed of ice crystals. High-level clouds are typically thin and white in appearance, but can appear in a magnificent array of colors when the sun is low on the horizon."*

We also need to understand that water vapor and small ice crystals exist also above these 6,000 m and differ only in their amount. Water vapor to create ice crystals releases latent heat from evaporation and melting on a height of 6,000 m. Also, this heat will more than likely go to space. When crystals become big enough, they will go down and cool the surrounding air by melting. They also will be a center for condensation of water vapor for mid-level clouds. It is always a dynamic process for water vapor and air with small droplets of water moving UP and DOWN. In this process, energy is released and goes to space more easily than from ground level.

*"**Mid-level clouds:** The bases of mid-level clouds typically appear between 6,500 to 20,000 feet (2,000 to 6,000 meters). Because of their lower altitudes, they are composed primarily of water droplets, however, they can also be composed of ice crystals when temperatures are cold enough."*

Mid-level clouds condense a lot of water vapor, but at the same time, the dynamic process of evaporation and condensation moves part of the water vapor UP to the next level and above. The cohesion process when water sticks to itself very easily unites small water droplets, which create droplets of rain. Droplets of rain while go toward land always partially evaporated and cool themselves and surrounding air while water vapor is going UP for the next condensation.

*"**Low-level clouds:** Low clouds are of mostly composed of water droplets since their bases generally lie below 6,500 feet (2,000 meters). However, when temperatures are cold enough, these clouds may also contain ice particles and snow."*

High, mid, and low-level clouds creation depends on the amount of evaporation from the ground (ocean) level and the speed of condensation with height. Humidity of air is always different in any place. Only if humidity will be close to 100% most of condensation is occur. It could be close to any source of evaporation. We could see fog close to land if humidity is high, or on every level of clouds. The speed of condensation with height depends on previous humidity, the temperature of air on a different level, and the speed of winds and their direction. These conditions could change, which type of clouds will be created first. If it will be low-level clouds, we must understand that the condensation of a big amount of water vapor will heat the air and bring it, along with water vapor, UP to the next level. In reality, we do not have strong lines that divide these clouds. It is always a dynamic process for the movement of water vapor and water droplets UP and DOWN with constant changes in their energy. The main direction of movement for that energy is UP, and properties of water create this possibility.

"<u>Vertically Developed Clouds</u> Probably the most familiar of the classified clouds is the cumulus cloud. Generated most commonly through either or <u>frontal lifting</u>, these clouds can grow t o heights in excess of 39,000 feet (12,000 meters), releasing incredible amounts of energy through the <u>condensation</u> of water vapor within the cloud itself."

Please pay attention that *"these clouds can grow to heights in excess of 39,000 feet (12,000 meters), releasing incredible amounts of energy through the <u>condensation</u> of water vapor within the cloud itself."*

It is not my discovery, it is knowledge for everyone on Wikipedia and is something that is understood by meteorologists as far back as the nineteenth century. Why scientists of the climate change decided from this fact that water vapor is responsible for climate change is a huge riddle of that science. Energy is released at the height of 12,000 m., despite that it is very cold there. What happened to that energy? Is it really that energy released at a height of 12,000 m will help create global warming? I can't explain this kind of logic in the science of climate change.

From Wikipedia, Virga http://en.wikipedia.org/wiki/Virga

This page was last modified on 25 March 2012.

Virga

In meteorology, *virga is an observable* streak *or shaft of* precipitation *that falls from a* cloud *but evaporates before reaching the ground. At high altitudes the precipitation falls mainly as* icecrystals *before melting and finally evaporating; this is usually due to compressional heating, because the* air pressure *increases closer to the ground. It is very common in the* desert *and in* temperate climates. *In North America, it is commonly seen in the* Western United States *and the* Canadian Prairies.

Virga can cause varying weather effects, because as rain is changed from liquid to vapor form, it removes heat from the air due to the high heat of vaporization *of water...*

Virga also has a role in seeding storm cells whereby small particles from one cloud are blown into neighboring supersaturated air and act as nucleation particles *for the next* thunderhead *cloud to begin forming.*

Virga is the observed evaporation of droplets of rain before they reach the ground. It helps to imagine millions of droplets, which are could be invisible because they are still very small and located far from each other. Despite we can't see them they are evaporated in the air and create a pendulum like movement of water in the upper troposphere. This process causes the creation of additional possibilities to transport heat from the air closer to the Earth's surface on more high level where heat energy will go to space more easily.

Let take some information from article: Latitude, 2012 http:// en.wikipedia.org/wiki/Altitude

The **troposphere** *is the lowest portion of Earth's atmosphere. It contains approximately 75% of the atmosphere's mass and 99% of its water vapor and aerosols.*

The Earth's atmosphere is divided into several altitude regions:

▲ *Troposphere—surface to 8,000 meters at the poles—18,000 meters at the equator, ending at the Tropopause.*

▲ *Stratosphere—troposphere to 50 kilometers.*

▲ *Mesosphere—Stratosphere to 85 kilometers.*

▲ *Thermosphere—Mesosphere to 675 kilometers*

▲ *Exosphere—Thermosphere to 10,000 kilometers.*

Back to article Web Curator: P. Kay Costulis, **2002 Clouds,**

http://asd-www.larc.nasa.gov/edu_act/clouds.html

Air is comprised mainly of nitrogen and oxygen, but also contains a small amount of water vapor. Clouds form when a parcel of air is cooled until the water vapor that it contains condenses to liquid form. Another way of saying this is that condensation (clouds) occur when an air parcel is **saturated** *with water vapor.*

> *The amount of moisture in a parcel of air is expressed in a variety of ways. The standard scientific measure is the partial pressure of water vapor. Partial pressure simply refers to the pressure exerted by only the water vapor part of the air parcel. The standard unit of measure is millibars (mb) and is typically a small fraction of total atmospheric pressure. The water vapor content can also be expressed as a mass mixing ratio, that is, the mass of water vapor per total mass of air. Mixing ratio is usually expressed as grams H20 per kilograms air.*

It is good to understand the point that the *"mixing ratio is usually expressed as grams H20 per kilograms air."* In case of saturation of vapor pressure in 1 kg of air, we will have around 25 grams of water vapor if the temperature of air is 25ºC. If the temperature of this air decreases to 0ºC, one kg of air could have only around 5 grams of water vapor. Twenty grams of water vapor in this case will be condensed into a water droplet for every kg of air.

Cloud Condensation Nuclei

Clouds may occur when air is cooled to near its dew point. There are three ways to cool air to its dew point:

1. advection of warm air over a cold surface

2. mixing air parcels of different temperature and moisture

3. lifting of air to higher levels

advection

The horizontal transfer of any atmospheric property by the wind.

⮞ *First, horizontal motion (**advection**) of warm and moist air over a cool surface will cause the air parcel to cool and condensation to occur. This is how advection fog forms.*

⮞ *Mixing parcels of different temperature and moisture can also result in cloudformation. The mixing cloud is another application of the Clausius-Clapeyron equation. Parcel A is warm and moist and Parcel B is cool and dry. When they are equally mixed, the final parcel has a vapor pressure equal to the saturation vapor pressure (es) and condensation occurs. Jet aircraft contrails are an example of this type of cloud.*

⮞ *A third way to cool air to its dew point is by lifting. Because pressure and accordingly, temperature, decrease rapidly with height, a rising parcel of air will cool rapidly*

In the atmosphere, clouds can form at relative humidity of less than 100%. This is due to the presence of minute (0.1 - 2 micrometers in radius) water- attracting (hygroscopic) particles. Water vapor will stick to, and condense on, these particles to form clouds -- hence the particles are termed cloud condensation nulcei (CCN).

CCN occur naturally in the atmosphere. Major sources of CCN are:

⋏ *volcanoes - dust and sulfate particles*

⋏ *oceans - sea salt particles*

⋏ *phytoplankton - sulfate particles*

⋏ *wildfires - soot and dust*

CCN can also result from man's activities. In particular, CCN occur as a byproduct of any combustion process. This includes motor vehicles emissions, industrial activity, and controlled fires (slash and burn agriculture).

The effect of CCN concentrations on climate is an area of continuing research. For example, if greenhouse-gas-induced-global warming occurs, sea surface temperature (SST) will increase. Will this result in increased emission of sulfates from phytoplankton? If so, will this significantly affect CCN concentrations over the oceans? Will increases in CCN concentrations result in increased cloud cover? Will this in turn lead to a cooling effect that will modulate the warming trend?"

It is a very interesting website (***Web Curator:*** P. Kay Costulis, ***2002 Clouds,*** http://asd-www.larc.nasa.gov/edu_act/clouds.html) about cloud formations, but even here, we could find the influence of today's science of climate change. There is not one sentence about the cooling effect of all properties of water, which by evaporation is cooling the air and helping convection forces because water vapor is lighter than most gases in the air. There is also not one sentence about how condensation releases heat and recreates convection forces.

At the same time, *"if greenhouse-gas-induced-global warming occurs, sea surface temperature (SST) will increase. Will this result in increased emission of sulfates from phytoplankton? If so, will this significantly affect CCN concentrations over the oceans?"*

The most interesting are the next two statements: *"Will increases in CCN concentrations result in increased cloud cover? Will this in turn lead to a cooling effect that will modulate the warming trend?"*

We have possibilities of increasing cloud cover by the emission of sulfates from phytoplankton. We also have possibilities of cooling effects by these clouds. It is a good example of how sophisticated the reasoning of climate scientists is. There are also some cooling effects of clouds in this article, while most scientists of climate change are saying that clouds create a heating, not cooling, effect.

Let look on statement fromBryan Walsh, 2010 , **Why CO2 Is the "Control Knob" for Global Climate Change,** *http://www. saskfarmersmarket.com/0-14490-why-co2-is-the-control-knob-for-global-climate-change.html*

"one argument you might hear from skeptics of manmade climate change is that CO2 is much less important as an atmospheric warming agent than water vapor. Here's how historical climatologist and skeptic Tim Ball summarizes the case for water vapor.

Water vapour is the most important greenhouse gas. If you get a fall evening and the sky is clear, heat will escape, the temperature will drop. If there's cloud cover, the heat is trapped by water vapour and the temperature stays warm. If you go to in Salah in southern Algeria, they recorded at noon 52°C. By midnight, it's -3.6°C. It's caused because there is very little water vapour in the atmosphere and is a demonstration of water vapour as the most important greenhouse gas.

As you can see from this statement climatologist Tim Ball is a skeptic of today science of climate change. He think that water vapor is more important greenhouse gas and because of that human activities do not responsible for climate change. Let's analyze this statement from Tim Ball from a different point of view. Is it true that In Salah has mostly nothing other than sand? Sand is not a good conductor of heat. .

Let take wikipedia article **"Heat transfer" 2012, http:// en.wikipedia.org/wiki/Heat_transfer**

Heat conduction, also called diffusion, is the direct microscopic exchange of kinetic energy of particles through the boundary between two systems. When an object is at a different temperature from another body or its surroundings, heat flows so that the body and the surroundings reach the same temperature, at which point they are in thermal equilibrium. Such spontaneous heat transfer always occurs from a region of high temperature to another region of lower temperature, as required by the second law of thermodynamics.

Thermal conductivity is the quantity of heat transmitted through a unit thickness in a direction normal to a surface of unit area, due to a unit temperature gradient under steady state conditions.

Unit of thermal conductivity

1 W/(m.K) = 1 W/(m.oC) = 0.85984 kcal/(hr.m.oC) = 0.5779 Btu/(ft.hr.oF).

Thermal conductivity of sand: dry—0.15-0.25; moist—0.25-2; saturated—2-4. As you can see, dry sand conductivity is too small to provide heat to the lower layers of sand in the daytime in Salah. It is the same since lower layers of sand will not give their heat to the surface at nighttime. As a result, we have very hot sand in the day, which heats the air, and very cold sand at night, which cools the air.

Do you remember: *"If you put a thermometer into barren, sandy soil you immediately get 120ºF. But just 1 meter away, where you have some surface cover, the temperature immediately drop to 109ºF,"* says Reij. *"And with a bit of luck, if you have vast area of regreening, the question is: might that begin to have positive impact on local rainfall as well?"*

If the surface has some cover by grass, the roots take more water, sometimes as deep as four meters below ground level. The same roots take some heat back to land from the grass or any other plants. It is a dynamic process in any living plant. It involves the transportation of energy from the Sun in all volumes of land from the surface to a few meters of deep roots. That is reason why a thermometer is showing lower temperatures under covered land and higher temperatures even just one meter away at daytime. At nighttime, the same roots of grass or any other plant will bring heat from deep land back to surface and also heat the air.

If water vapor is playing some role in this situation, as Tim Ball suggests, it will be that water vapor from grass at nighttime in cold air condenses to water droplets and additionally releases energy to heat the air. It is the properties of roots and their abilities to bring water from deeper layers of land in the daytime as well as at night. These are the same properties of roots to take extra heat from vegetation back to land at daytime and heat vegetation at night by sun energy, which roots collect in the land during a day.

Let's look at this subject from a root's point of view.

David Whiting, Michael Roll, Lary Vickerman, 2011, **Colorado State University Extension,** http://www.cmg.colostate.edu/gardennotes/132.pdf

"CMG GardenNotes #132

Plant Structures: Roots

It is difficult to predict root spread of any plant. Under favorable growing conditions, the typical root spread of a tree includes:

- *90-95% in top 36 inches*

- *50% in top 12 inches*

- *Spreads 2-3 times tree's height or canopy (drip-line) spread*

On compacted clayey soils, the typical root spread of trees includes:

- *90-95% in top 12 inches or less*

- *50% in top 4 inches*

- *Potentially spreads five plus times the tree's height or canopy (drip-line) spread*

Some plants are genetically programmed to have very deep, spreading root systems

(i.e., they are more tolerant of low soil oxygen levels). This growth habit is an environmental adaptation. Examples include bindweed and prairie grasses.

Soil type is a key factor in water penetration and root uptake. Where soil allows, the primary water extraction depth extends to:

corn will only start growing its roots. During the last month, corn will almost stop evaporating water completely.

From Wikipedia:

Let look in article Wikipedia, 2012, Root, http://en.wikipedia.org/wiki/Root

> "The distribution of vascular plant roots within soil depends on plant form, the spatial and temporal availability of water and nutrients, and the physical properties of the soil. The deepest roots are generally found in deserts and temperate coniferous forests; the shallowest in tundra, boreal forest and temperate grasslands. The deepest observed living root, at least 60 m below the ground surface, was observed during the excavation of an open-pit mine in Arizona, USA. Some roots can grow as deep as the tree is high. The majority of roots on most plants are however found relatively close to the surface where nutrient availability and aeration are more favourable for growth. Rooting depth may be physically restricted by rock or compacted soil close below the surface, or by anaerobic soil conditions._

Rooting Depth Records

Species	Location	Maximum rooting depth (m)	References
Boscia albitrunca	Kalahari desert	68	Jennings (1974)
Juniperus monosperma	Colorado Plateau	61	Cannon (1960)
Eucalyptus sp.	Australian forest	61	Jennings (1971)
Acacia erioloba	Kalahari desert	60	Jennings (1974)
Prosopis juliflora	Arizona desert	53.3	Phillips (1963)

As you can see, roots can provide nutrition and water to their plants from ground level up to 68 m deep. It is like oceans of roots on the continents and human activities, of course, changed these oceans. Human activities reduce the evaporation of vegetation provided by roots on the arable land of continents.

Area of USA: At 3.79 million square miles (9.83 million km²).

9,830,000 km²=9,830,000,000,000 m²=98,300,000,000,000,000 cm².

Normal pressure is 1 kg/cm². This means that every square centimeter of air weighs around 1 kg.

The air above the USA area weighs around 98,300,000,000,000,000 kg.

In every kg of air during the summer time, with humidity around 50 %, there is around 12.5 g of water in the form of water vapor.

If we increase the amount of water in every kg of air with 5 g (0.005 kg), there will be an additional 491,500,000,000,000 kg of water vapor.

Imagine how this additional water vapor will influence the climate in North America.

North America is only one continent between the Pacific and Atlantic oceans. Climate in North America will influence the climate from Japan to France. That is more than half of the Northern Hemisphere.

Let's look at the properties of water which could cool the atmosphere.

1. We need 539Kcal to evaporate 1 kg of water. It is cool air close to the surface of evaporation—oceans, seas, rivers, lakes, leaves of trees, bushes, grass, etc.

2. Water vapor is lighter than most gases in the air and helps convection forces bring ALL GASES UP.

3. The cooling of air with height stops convection forces around 500 m from sea level. We could see it in smoke from chimneys of power plants. In the green section of every magazine you could easily find pictures of this. Despite the temperature in an oven more than 500ºC, very soon we could see that vertical movement of smoke become almost horizontal.

4. Only partial condensation of water vapor releases energy to heat the parcels of surrounding air, including GHG. It is this property of water that recreates convection and helps bring all gases on the next level UP from land or oceans.

5. Droplets of water in rain, as cleaner water, takes almost all particles of black carbon and other aerosols from the atmosphere and brings them to land and oceans. This process decreases the heating of the atmosphere by trapping direct sun radiation in black carbon.

6. Only new snow is covered in soot from the old snow on the land and ice in oceans. This process increases the reflection of direct sun radiation back to space, and only properties of water could provide it.

7. Droplets of water partially solve all gases, including GHG, and bring them down as nutrition. It is mostly the properties of water that clean the atmosphere from GHG and reduce them.

8. 99% of water vapor condensed in the upper troposphere. If we remember that these properties of water release energy in the process and its energy close to space, we will understand that it helps cool the atmosphere.

9. Band of IR radiation for H2 O and CO2 is different. That means that if CO2 is present after the upper troposphere, most of IR radiation from water vapor going to space does not trap in CO2 molecules.

Let look in book *Philander George, 2011, Our Affair With El Niño*

1. *"Earth with no atmosphere-, the average surface temperature of Earth would be -18º C (0º F), far colder than the average temperature of our Earth, which is 15º C (59º F). Worse, the surface would cool down to around -160º C (-250º F) soon after the sunset.*

2. *Earth with a static atmosphere and no ocean. If the Earth had a static atmosphere with the same gases it has now, but with little water vapor and no ocean, the average surface temperature of Earth would be 67º C (153º F).*

3. *Earth with an atmosphere and ocean Earth has an atmosphere and ocean, and the average surface temperature is a comfortable 15º C (59º F). Water evaporates from the ocean and land, cooling the surface. Winds carry the water vapor to other latitudes, and sometimes high up into the air, where heat is released when the vapor condenses to water.*

As you can see, George Philander confirms that water vapor actually cools the air. In the second paragraph, the average surface temperature of Earth would be 67º C (153º F). In the third paragraph, the average surface temperature is a comfortable 15º C (59º F).

George Philander confirms:

"Water evaporates from the ocean and land, cooling the surface. Winds carry the water vapor to other latitudes, and sometimes high up into the air, where heat is released when the vapor condenses to water."

PROPERTIES OF WATER ARE THE BEST COOLER OF THE AIR!

Because they are lighter than most gases, water vapor is going up to cloud level, where the energy is taken by evaporation being released. But it happens 2–7 miles from ocean (land) level which is where this energy can more easily escape to space. If any greenhouse gas (GHG) molecule traps infrared (IR) radiation, its energy has great possibilities to evaporate some molecule from closest water droplets AND THE VAPOR WILL GO UP. Evaporation of water from the ground, and water DROPLETS in the air, actually cool the air. Water in droplets is the cleanest water in nature and because of that, they solve all gases in the air, including greenhouse gases. It means that droplets of water could trap all range waves of IR radiation, which could trap any type of GHG we have in the air around those droplets. When rain droplets from the air go to the ground, it will be partially or COMPLETELY evaporated. This process creates a pendulum-like process of evaporation and condensation in the air. I have not seen in scientific literature how many times the pendulum works before rain droplets will come to the Earth's surface. But everyone could see how fog tails after jets sometime disappear, and if you have patience, you also could see the same for small clouds. Evaporation of these droplets without any doubt will take energy. Evaporation of water droplets also cools them. Without any doubt, we could imagine how it is working by feeling rain droplets, which even in a hot summer, is cooler than the surrounding air before rain. One kg of water takes 539Kcal of energy to evaporate, but returns to the surface just as cold, despite the fact that its energy could boil more than 6 kg of water (in summertime, from 20º C to 100ºC.) Where is this energy going? It dissipates to space in a pendulum-like process of condensation and evaporation in the air from the surface to the cloud level.

The annual mean of global concentration of water vapor would yield about 25 mm of liquid water over the entire surface of the Earth if it were to instantly condense. However, the mean annual precipitation for the planet is about one meter, which indicates a rapid turnover of water in the air. In this process, many droplets of rain, or other droplets of water in the atmosphere, makes the turnover not even able to reach the surface of land. If we could somehow calculate all water which goes up and down during the year, it will be significantly more than one meter.

Why do all models give results from 3.8º to 8.1º? Is it not suspicious? Why is it possible that water, which needs huge amounts of energy to evaporate and releases that energy mostly on cloud level because water vapor is lighter than most gases in the air, suddenly becomes the main reason for climate change?

It is a shame for scientists, our mass media, and all governments in the world to fool themselves and the population with dogmatic science without any scientific reasons.

In *The End of the Long Summer*, Dianne Dumanoski wrote that scientists in 1974 concluded that CFCs accumulation in the lower atmosphere posed no hazard.

This is what the Internet had to say about CFCs:

McFarland and Kaye,1992, "Chlorofluorocarbons and Ozone."

http://www.ciesin.org/TG/OZ/cfcozn.html

Chlorofluorocarbons (CFCs), along with other chlorine- and bromine-containing compounds, have been implicated in the accelerated depletion of ozone in the Earth's stratosphere. CFCs were developed in the early 1930s and are used in a variety of industrial, commercial, and household applications. These substances are non-toxic, non-flammable, and non-reactive with other chemical compounds. These desirable safety characteristics, along with their stable thermodynamic properties, make them ideal for many applications--as coolants for commercial and home refrigeration units, aerosol propellants, electronic cleaning solvents, and blowing agents. Production and use of Chlorofluorocarbons experienced nearly uninterrupted growth as demand for products requiring their use continued to rise.

Not until 1973 was chlorine found to be a catalytic agent in ozone destruction. Catalytic destruction of ozone removes the odd oxygen species [atomic oxygen (O) and ozone (O3)] while leaving chlorine unaffected. This process was known to be potentially damaging to the ozone layer, but conclusive evidence of stratospheric ozone loss was not discovered until 1984.

If during 40 years, the consensus of scientists couldn't recognize the most dangerous properties of CFCs for civilization, why do we need to put such a huge amount of attention on the consensus of scientists about the reason for global warming and how to fight back if it is real? It is a very serious question because in every dispute, we hear and/or read about the consensus of scientists. Yes, scientists are more informed than everyone else is; but please forgive me, what about Aristotle and Copernicus, or Newton and Einstein, and the many other scientists whose discoveries confront the consensus of scientists of their time. Persons who confront the opinion of the consensus of scientists made, make, and will make differences.

From *Earth Science*, Baron's Educational Series, Inc. 2001:

"Solar radiation reaches the upper atmosphere at a fairly constant rate of about 200 kilocalories per minute/square meter. About 1/3 of this radiation is reflected back into space mostly by clouds."

IS IT NOT WATER VAPOR THAT CREATES CLOUDS?

IS IT NOT CLOUDS THAT REFLECT 1/3 OF SUN RADIATION TO SPACE?

WHAT IS BETTER THAN WATER VAPOR TO TRANSPORT THE HUGE ENERGY OF EVAPORATION CLOSE TO SPACE?

WHAT IS BETTER THAN CONDENSATION AND EVAPORATION PROCESSES BRING ENERGY OF ALL GASES IN PARCEL OF AIR CLOSE TO UPPER TROPOSPHERE?

HOW MANY TIMES IS THIS PENDULUM OF TRANSPORTATION OF ENERGY CLOSE TO SPACE WORKING?

PLEASE REPEAT AFTER THAT ABOUT THE INFLUENCES OF CO2 AND OTHER GHG AS MAIN PLAYERS IN GLOBAL WARMING.

AND IF YOU DOUBT IN THAT, PLEASE START YOUR DOUBT IN IMPLEMENTATION OF CUP & TRADE, SOLAR

CELLS, WIND, NUCLEAR, AND GEOTHERMAL SOURCE OF ENERGY AS THE BEST TOOL TO FIGHT GLOBAL WARMING. THAY ARE DISASTROUS FOR THE ECONOMY AND FOR THE ENVIRONMENT.

GLOBAL WARMING COULD BE REAL.

THE EXPLANATION ABOUT THE REASON FOR THAT IS WRONG. AND BECAUSE OF THAT, WE ARE USING THE WRONG TOOLS TO FIGHT GLOBAL WARMING.

"Human activities increase GHG in air. In hot air, there will be more water vapor. Water vapor is GHG, therefore the temperature will rise."

This nonsensical feedback absolutely ignores the other properties of water. Water vapor that is lighter than most gases in the air is always going up to cloud level and above. The condensation of water releases heat energy 2–7 miles close to space, which is where that energy is going to space more easily than from sea level. On Mount Everest, there is always snow. In Florida, which is located on the same latitude, it is always hotter. It is despite that huge energy of condensation in the process of creating clouds that must heat the air on Mount Everest, especially if the density of air there is not as big as it is at ocean level.

We have simple solutions to regulate the average temperatures on the Earth during any increase of energy, Milankovich's cycles, and other predictable cycles of the Earth's temperature. Sunspots with their cycle last 11 years. Earth orbit ellipse, whose shape changes on the 100,000-year cycle. The tilt of the Earth on its axis with a cycle of 42,000 years. The wobble of Earth on its axis with a cycle of 22,000 years- all these processes, of course will influence the climate on the earth. Mankind has only one tool to keep condition on the Earth as good as possible. It is only evaporation of water on continents. Increasing amount of evaporation of water on continents close to evaporation of water in oceans could help mankind to survive almost in any conditions, which history of land had.

Let analyze article:

Hansen James, Solomon Susan, Daniel John, Sanford Todd, Murphy Daniel, Plattner Gian-Kasper, Friedlingstein Pierre, 2010 Persistence of climate changes due to a range of greenhouse gases.

"Abstract

Emissions of a broad range of greenhouse gases of varying lifetimes contribute to global climate change. Carbon dioxide displays exceptional persistence that renders its warming nearly irreversible for more than 1,000 y. Here we show that the warming due to non-CO2 greenhouse gases, although not irreversible, persists notably longer than the anthropogenic changes in the greenhouse gas concentrations themselves. We explore why the persistence of warming depends not just on the decay of a given greenhouse gas concentration but also on climate system behavior, particularly the timescales of heat transfer linked to the ocean. For carbon dioxide and methane, nonlinear optical absorption effects also play a smaller but significant role in prolonging the warming. In effect, dampening factors that slow temperature increase during periods of increasing concentration also slow the loss of energy from the Earth's climate system if radiative forcing is reduced. Approaches to climate change mitigation options through reduction of greenhouse gas or aerosol emissions therefore should not be expected to decrease climate change impacts as rapidly as the gas or aerosol lifetime, even for short-lived species; such actions can have their greatest effect if undertaken soon enough to avoid transfer of heat to the deep ocean."

Oh, you see what we have in the future a *"transfer of heat to the deep ocean."* If one would say that the properties of water are the best thermostat on the Earth, could he or she receive any science degree? Of course not, it is the knowledge from the nineteenth century. If you put 1,000,000,000 data into a computer model, it will look very scientific. It also will be very inclusive for the next generation of scientists which could put in additional data and receive new results, such as, *"transfer of heat to the deep ocean."* We need to hurry with the reduction of carbon dioxide and another GHG, otherwise heat from deep oceans will create GLOBAL OCEANS WARMING PROBLEMS. Seven authors that are from Colorado, Switzerland,

France, United Kingdom, are peer reviewed and are *"edited by James E. Hansen, Goddard Institute for Space Studies, New York, NY, and approved August 31, 2010"*. Do they really believe what they discover, or is it fairy international tales for a first grader about how GHG will help underwater volcano to heat oceans?

Let's return to land problems.

"Destruction of the Earth's thin living cover is proceeding at a rate and on a scale unparalleled in history, and when that thin cover -- the soil -- is gone, the fertile regions where it formerly lay will be uninhabitable deserts." That could have been written yesterday, but in fact it's more than 60 years old -- from The Rape of the Earth: A World Survey of Soil Erosion, by Jacks and Whyte, published in 1939."

The Industrial Revolution, which used mostly fossil fuels as its source of energy, brought destruction to the air by releasing additional GHG and other pollutants. The same Industrial Revolution creates *"Destruction of the Earth's thin living cover is proceeding at a rate and on a scale unparalleled in history, and when that thin cover -- the soil -- is gone, the fertile regions where it formerly lay will be uninhabitable deserts."*

Why was desertification of the soil skipped by Cullen and other scientists of climate change? This was in 1939, and hundreds of years before, and this is still happening all around the world today, and will be in the future. It is happening to millions of square kilometers in the world and means nothing to scientists of climate change.

"Today, the deserts are spreading at the rate of five million hectares a year worldwide (not yet quite as fast as the forests are vanishing). A third of the world's land surface is at risk from desertification, threatening the livelihoods of more than 850 million people (United Nations Development Program)."

How is it possible that one United Nations program writing about the reason for desertification, which does not correlate with the science of climate change, from one another, under the United Nations' direction?

"The United Nations Framework Convention on Climate Change *is an international environmental treaty that was aimed at stabilizing*

greenhouse gas concentrations in the atmosphere at a level that would "prevent dangerous anthropogenic interference with the climate system."

*"American researcher J. Russell Smith charted how this disastrous progression could be reversed by using special trees, especially in the hills. "When we develop an agriculture that fits the land, it will become an almost endless vista of green, crop-yielding trees," he wrote in **Tree Crops: A Permanent Agriculture** (1929)."*

"Agriculture in mountainous, rocky or dry regions is a disaster, but trees are salvation," wrote Fritz Schumacher, author of "Small is Beautiful: Economics As If People Mattered" and founder of the Intermediate Technology Development Group."

"But forestry projects often don't work very well, especially when they're centrally planned. One project achieved only 2.5% of the production claimed. (See Ipil-ipil, the 'magic tree'.)"

"And "re-forestation" often replaces a mature forest rich in biodiversity with a biologically simple plantation."

"It can be a different matter when projects are mounted at the local level – forestry as if people mattered. There are many such projects, quietly planting trees where there were none, bringing multiple benefits to the local people who plant them and tend them, and to everybody else too, though you don't hear much about it."

Re-forestation, as well as other not-for-profit directions, will always be on the low level of development. Only if we will find economic reasons to grow forests we could make a real difference in our solutions.

> *"Trees, soil and water*
> *Trees for deserts: HDRA*
> *Trees and forests -- resources for schools*
>
> *"Oracle'ThinkQuest*
>
> *Educational Foundation.*
>
> *Depending on the species of tree, bark has different characteristics and functions. It provides trees with essential structural support,*

conducts nutrients from the leaves down to the roots, and offers protection from wood-boring insects and twig-gnawing mammals. In some cases, however, the bark itself becomes a food source, attracting animals such as porcupines which feed on the bark during the winter.

All trees have bark of some form and color. Some is smooth and shiny or papery, some is rough, thick and ridged. The variety of bark coloration is as diverse as its textures--tree trunks come in every shade from light silvery-white to deep orange-brown."

It is a very important point that *"bark has different characteristics and functions. It provides trees with essential structural support, conducts nutrients from the leaves down to the roots..."*

Bark conducts nutrients from the leaves down to the roots. We have two directions of movement of liquid in trees—UP with water and nutrients from soil, and DOWN with nutrients from the leaves to roots. In context, which is important to us in this book, this means that sun energy is dissipated by roots inside the soil and could be as deep as the deep roots of trees or other vegetation.

These roots could be 60 m deep, or could be 10 cm. Like in trees and many other types of vegetation, roots could live for hundreds of years or only one year, as in most crops' vegetation. In the case that they live many years, they evaporate water all year, even in the wintertime. In the case that they live only one year, vegetation evaporates water during spring, summer, and fall times according to their vegetation period. For most crops, the vegetation period is no more than three to four months. Before and after that, the soil behaves like sand in deserts and heats or cools the air only by conductivity of dry, wet, or saturated soil. The role of roots in this case is close to zero.

"There is a major difference between the wood of most coniferous and broadleaved trees. Broadleaved trees have 'pipes' (called vessels) running through the wood to carry nutrients between the roots and the leaves. Coniferous trees don't have these vessels. Instead, nutrients are moved up the trunk through small chains of special

cells within the wood, and down the trunk from the leaves to the roots through cells in the bark. The vessels in broadleaved trees are many times larger than the chains of cells in coniferous trees (which can be as small as .2 millimeters), and therefore nutrients can flow much faster: sap can move at rates of 20 meters an hour in some oak trees, compared to only half a meter during the same amount of time in coniferous trees."

Nature provides biodiversity not only to feed different appetites, but also to cool the trees and other vegetation differently in different weather conditions. Mankind activities mostly do not correlate with these achievements by nature; sometimes it is by necessity to feed the population, but mostly it is because of a lack of education. If we destroy oceans of roots, which cool and heat the air on millions and millions of square kilometers, and scientists of climate change did not and do not look at the influence of these mankind activities on climate change and put their attention only on GHG, it is the fault of these scientists' blindness. It is a shame for our science of climate change. The possibilities of the computerization of millions of influential reasons for climate change provide wrong directions for scientists. It is a huge job to collect data and put them into a computer and maybe because of that stops the abilities of these scientists to analyze reasons and results.

"Tree roots are the essential framework for preventing soil erosion. Without roots to hold the soil in place, forest slopes simply wash away. Tree roots can extend great distances, and in some cases, roots from separate trees (of the same species) can "graft" themselves together. Roots from many trees can grow together into a single enormous network that supports many individual trees. Thus, when nutrients from a healthy tree are brought down into the roots, they may be "stolen" by a different individual tree that gets very little sunlight. Stumps connected to this network of roots can remain alive by receiving nutrients from the other trees."

These statements are absolutely true for perennial grass in virgin soil. It is easy to destroy the root system in soil and receive instant erosion, which we have seen in many places on the Earth.

We destroyed it with machinery and received as many GHG as we did erosion. All developed nations, including the USA, are living in an area with more than enough precipitation. Maybe this reason is a dominant point as to why the erosion of land is not so visible. But even in these places, erosion is a fact without any illusion. We still have enough water to grow the roots of most vegetation during three to four months, but we don't have roots to take water from the land during the whole year by evaporation. This situation creates droughts in many areas and flooding in others, more than all GHG in the world. **Sometimes very little differences in the humidity of air could bring rain in dry areas.** Growing trees in Salah, Algeria and Sahel, Nigeria could bring these little differences, if we would support these directions on all arable lands on the Earth. Using machinery in these directions will also increase GHG in the atmosphere, but the result will be completely different.

For food production, it will be better to reduce the areas for crops and increase the areas for forests all around the world. It will help to escape drought and more rain could help feed mankind better than more areas for crops without rain. Fruit and nut trees could not only restore rainfall, but could also provide food for animals and people. It is the simple logic of scientists like Chris Reij, Gianniny, and many others that must prevail against the aggressive logic of scientists of climate change.

Let's look at history for a moment.

From Wikipedia:"Sahel, This page was last modified on 11 April 2012 http://en.wikipedia.org/wiki/Sahel

> *"The first instances of domestication of plants for agricultural purposes in Africa occurred in the Sahel region circa 5000 BC, when* <u>sorghum</u> *and* <u>African rice</u> *began to be cultivated.*

> *Around 4000 BC the climate of the Sahara and the Sahel started to become drier at an exceedingly fast pace. This climate change caused lakes and rivers to shrink rather significantly and caused increasing* <u>desertification</u>. *(O'Brien, Patrick K., ed (2005).*

Oxford Atlas of World History. New York: Oxford University Press. pp. 22–23.

It is interesting that 1000 years of domestication of sorghum and rice was enough to change the climate in Sahara and Sahel. If we suggest that the area for these plants grow was not as fast as with today's machinery, 1000 years is not such a big time period.

What is difference in nature between domestication and wild vegetation?

Let look at Project"Interactive Agricultural Ecological Atlas of Russia and neighboring countries", 2003-2009

http://www.agroatlas.ru/en/content/cultural/Sorghum_bicolor_K/

"Sorghum is a short-day crop. It thrives with 10–11 hours of sunlight a day. A shorter photoperiod results in a vegetation period three weeks longer prior to flowering and almost six weeks longer prior to full flowering. Many sorghum varieties do not flower at all with insufficient light. Fast-ripening varieties' vegetation period lasts 90–105 days; mid-season varieties' vegetation period lasts 106–120 days; and slow-ripening varieties' vegetation period lasts 120– 130 days or more."

The difference is simple—the vegetation period changed from 360 days for wild vegetation to 90–130 days for sorghum.

Let go back to *"Trees, soil and water, trees for deserts: HDR4 Trees and forests -- resources for schools, Oracle'ThinkQuest,' Educational Foundation."The leaves are where "food" is created for the tree. Leaves are green because they contain a chemical called chlorophyll. This chemical allows the plant to manufacture sugars from carbon dioxide and water in a process called photosynthesis. Most leaves have a relatively tough, waxy, water-proof coating which protect them from hungry insects. It is only through the coating's tiny pores, called "stomata", that the required carbon dioxide can enter the leaf.*

During photosynthesis, plants capture red and blue light wavelengths, and use their energy to combine the component atoms of water with carbon dioxide. The plant uses the resulting sugars for its own growth. Oxygen is simply a by-product of the reaction. All green plants use the chemical chlorophyll for photosynthesis. In fact, all plants are green because of chlorophyll -- it absorbs the red and blue light wavelengths, and only reflects green.

The stomata in the leaves, however, also let water vapor escape from the leaves. While this does work to cool leaves in the hot sun, plants in dry areas have fewer stomata or keep them closed for most of the day. This slows this rate of water loss (called transpiration) and prevents dehydration. In most trees, the fact that much more liquid is being moved upwards from the roots to the leaves than in the opposite direction is obvious when you consider that cells within the entire outer trunk carry nutrients upwards, but only the thin layer of bark carries them downwards.

It is a riddle for me why botanists, with their knowledge, are so silent on the madness of today's science of climate change. Why does no one correlate their knowledge with the big picture of climate change? Why are they so shy to stop the flooding of wrong sciences in world institutions? Why does no one stop Kyoto, Copenhagen, or Durban?

From article in Wikipedia, *Last Updated: 09/30/2002* "Clouds"

http://asd-www.larc.nasa.gov/edu_act/clouds.html

"The most common ways to lift a parcel of air are: buoyancy, topographic lifting, and convergence.

Buoyant lifting results from surface heating. This is a common manner of cloud formation in the summer. Buoyancy lifting is also called convection and occurs when local warm areas heat the air near the surface. The warm air is less dense than the surrounding air and rises. This rising air will eventually cool to its dew point and form a fair-weather cumulus cloud."

"Buoyant lifting always accompanies by partially condensation of water vapor, which heat the parcel of air and because of that recreate convection forces."

It is not my statements; they are from Wikipedia. It is knowledge for everyone. The condensation of water is responsible for lifting air close to the upper troposphere and UP.

It is simple logic: the bigger the height of a parcel of air in the atmosphere, the easier the way to space for the energy in this parcel. This parcel contains all gases, including GHG; therefore, all gases will easily send their energy with height to space. Why do we need computer models if they are completely away from this simple logic and trying to fool us into the opposite direction that water vapor as GHG is the most dangerous for our civilization?

"Air that is forced into, or over, a topographic barrier will also rise and cool to form clouds. This occurs near mountain ranges. For example, warm and moist air from the Gulf of Mexico can be pushed northwestward and up the eastern slope of the Rockies to form extensive cloud decks.

Finally, lifting occurs where there is large scale convergence of air. Cold fronts are a location of strong convergence as cold, dense southward moving air displaces warmer air. Convergence can also occur on smaller scales along the leading edge of the sea or bay breeze boundaries.

*The formation of clouds is an application of the First Law of Thermodynamics. According to the First Law, a change in the internal energy of a system can be due to the addition (or loss) of heat or to the work done on (or by) the system. In the atmosphere system, the change of internal energy is measured as a change in temperature and the work done is manifested as a change in pressure. Because air is a relatively poor conductor of heat energy, the assumption is made that the parcel of air upon which work is being done is insulated from the surrounding environment. This is the **adiabatic** assumption. For a rising air parcel, the change in internal energy is therefore due entirely to pressure work with no addition or loss of heat to the surrounding environment. A simple relationship for temperature change for a rising parcel of air can then be determined. This change of temperature with height is the dry adiabatic lapse rate of -9.8oC per kilometer.*

(adiabatic-the process without transfer of heat, compression results in warming, expansion results in cooling.)

Air is, of course, not entirely dry and always contains some water vapor which can condense as the air parcel rises and cools. Condensation creates clouds and affects the temperature and vertical motion of the parcel. During condensation, heat is released (latent heat of condensation). This addition of heat to the system violates the adiabatic assumption. The rate of cooling of an ascending air parcel undergoing condensation is, therefore, less than for dry air. The lapse rate for air under these conditions is the moist adiabatic lapse rate and is approximately -5oC per kilometer... "

Please read and reread these simple explanation *"During condensation, heat is released.*

It is difficult to imagine, that Cullen, Dessler, Hansen, Solomon, and thousands of other climate scientists, which dedicate their entire lives to the science of climate change, do not know about the simple, and so powerful, forces in nature. But, if "debate is over," how can they be against their own dogma?

*"A **sea-breeze** (or **onshore breeze**) is a* <u>wind</u> *from the sea that develops over land near coasts. It is formed by increasing temperature differences between the land and water which create a pressure minimum over the land due to its relative warmth and forces higher pressure, cooler air from the sea to move inland. Generally, air temperature gets cooler relative to nearby locations as one moves closer to a large body of water."*

It is so simple: *"Generally, air temperature gets cooler relative to nearby locations as one moves closer to a large body of water."*

In the case of oceans, scientists of climate change could make speculations that deep water has the inertia of heating huge masses of water, and because of that, it is cooler. In nature, we have a lot of small lakes with water that is no deeper than one or two meters.

Close to these small lakes, it is also cooler. Why is that? Oh, it is my biggest achievement in today's science. Nobody knew it, only me.

It is..., it is..., of course, it is EVAPORATION! EVAPORATION COOLS THE AIR! WHY HAS NO ONE MENTIONED IT?

I hope you understand my sarcasm, but billions of people are fooled by today's science of climate change for some reason and forget that they prefer to spend their vacations *"closer to a large body of water"* and that make them happier.

*" A **sea-breeze** (or **onshore breeze**) is a wind from the sea that develops over land near coasts."*

If a sea-breeze develops over land near coast let's look at the North American continent between the Atlantic, Pacific, and Arctic oceans. It's shaped like a triangle with one angle located close to the Equator and the opposite side close to the Arctic Ocean. In the summertime, sea-breeze, or ocean-breeze, shows movement of air from the Atlantic and Pacific to the continental area. As a result of the cold Pacific, warm Atlantic (Gulf Stream), and the hot continent, most winds are from San Diego to Montreal by direction. **These winds transport energy from the Equator to the North Pole.** If we increase the evaporation of water on this continent, the power of the ocean-breeze from the Pacific to the Atlantic will reduce. It will not only reduce the transportation of energy from the Equator to the North Pole (reason for global warming (cooling)), it will also reduce the power of hurricanes.

It will turn moisture from the Atlantic to Africa. It's mean from Atlantic ocean to Sahal in Algeria and Sahel in Nigeria. If population in Sahal and Sahel will help nature by growing additional trees, there will be enough humidity to recreate rains in these dry areas. It is logic of scientists like Gianniny and Reij. Their logic must prevail in today science, despite they represent maybe less than 0.01% of scientists.

North America is a special continent on the Earth. It is possible to change climate tendency in the world by changing the evaporation on this continent.

The*"biggest irony"* of our times is to blame water for global warming, despite the fact that its properties are cooling, not heating, the air and the evaporation of it could be used for our prosperity. We destroyed oceans of roots, which created by nature. It helps before Industrial Revolution to keep higher levels of evaporation on continents. This evaporation helps till 1850 prevent the global warming of today's level. We must restore evaporation on continents to at least the level it was before the Industrial Revolution.

It is not a difficult task.

We could evaporate even more water to achieve our goals. Brazil Rainforest receives close to 3 meters of rain every year. It is three times more than average amount of rain in oceans. Leaves of trees provide more evaporation from unit of area, than oceans.

We could also say that it is a very profitable direction to change the climate on the Earth. We could make changes during a few years and create jobs in North American countries despite globalization. It is not only the cheapest, but it also the most profitable way to fight climate change in the world. If we put our efforts into the right directions, we could do more than nature did before the Industrial Revolution. To increase evaporation on North American continents, we could restore the oceans of roots on a continental level. Also, we could pump water from flood areas to drought areas. Energy, which right now we spend after disasters to restore houses and other properties, which we use to live, is better to use to prevent disasters of any forms. In most cases, the evaporation of water is the best tool for prevention any kind of weather disasters.

North America is the best continent to start.

Energy Is The Main Force Of Our Civilization

Let look at article:"Energy in the UnitEnergy in the United Statesed States"This page was last modified on 11 April 2012

http://www.earth-policy.org/datacenter/xls/update83_2.xls

USA Total Consumption until 2009 in MTOE (Million Tons of Oil Equivalent)

> *1990—1914; 1991—1929.6; 1992—1967,5; 1993—2000,9;*
>
> *1994—2041,3; 1995—2067,3; 1996—2118.4; 1997—2140,7;*
>
> *1998—2167,2; 1999—2215,9; 2000—2279,6; 200—2235,8;*
>
> *2002—2270,6; 2003—2265,2; 2004—2311; 2005—2324,6;*
>
> *2006—2304,5; 2007—2340,5; 2008—2301,4; 2009—2201,4*
>
> *CAGR = Compound Annual Growth Rate Note: Total energy include: coal, gas, oil, electricity, heat and biomass, 2000-2009-- 0.4%*

Of course, we need to save energy if we can. Scientists of climate change care more about GHG and offer very childish directions on how to reduce them. How smart is this advice following the logic of 98% of scientists:

Save energy at home.
Choose energy efficient lighting, appliances.
Insulate your house.
Conserve your water.
Switch to green power.
Telecommute from home.
Reduce air travel.
Consume less.
Reduce, reuse, recycle.
Modify your diet to reduce meat.
Buy local...

People are smart enough to choose lighting and appliances and insulate their houses, but conserve your water, switch to green power, telecommute, reduce air travel, consume less, modify your diet to reduce meat... These are amendments for poor people which want to be poor forever. If we put our energy to recreate all sources of evaporation, which were, before 1850, all forests, lakes, etc., we will also increase the amount of GHG in the air, but we will return the climate to the same level as it was in 1850. Additional rain will bring the same GHG to land; not only reducing the amount of them in the air, but it will also feed the vegetation.

The best tools to evaporate water on continents are trees. In a famous Reagan slogan *"trees are more pollutant than automobiles,"* we have part of the truth. Forest reflects only 3–5% of direct sun radiation. Why, in this case, do we need forests? It is only because of evaporation, which cools the atmosphere and mild climates everywhere. The efficiency of photosynthesis and most solar cells are approximately the same, around 1%. The other part of sun energy heats the air. In the case of trees, this energy evaporates water and cools the air. In the case of solar panels, it heats the air and increases the possibilities of climate change.

Trees collect sun energy during hundreds of years without any batteries.

Let's look at some very important information from this next book:

FLANNERY, TIM, 2006, THE WEATHER MAKERS

1. " *Forests contain much more carbon than does grass, and they also absorb more sunlight (having different albedo) and produce more water vapor, which affects cloud formation* ".

2. *"Mature forests don't take in much CO2 they are in balance, releasing CO2 as old vegetation rots, then absorbing it as new grows. For these reasons the world largest forests-the coniferous forests of Siberia and Canada, and the tropical rainforests are not good carbon sinks, but new vigorously forests are."(p. 32).*

If old vegetation rots and releases CO2 into the atmosphere anyway, there is nothing wrong with burning old trees before they start to rot.

I understand the reader's frustration; I started with growing trees to save the planet from climate change by increasing the evaporation of water on continents, and after a few sentences, off offer to burn trees. But ask yourself these questions:

Why do we need to burn trees?

Is it to save the planet?

Is it for energy?

Are there enough forests for our energy needs?

I will try to answer on all these questions.

Let's analyze "HOW WE USE ENERGY AND WHAT WE MUST CHANGE".

Transportation System

The efficiency of the engine in most cars moving by gasoline is around 30%. The efficiency of gasoline production is less than 45%. This means that the real efficiency of car movement is around 13.5%. If a person (100 kg.), mostly alone, is driving in a car (2,000 kg.), it means that the real efficiency of movement of this person in this car is less than 0.67%.

Perhaps the mass (m) of the car is 2,000 kg, the mass of the driver is 100 kg, and the speed (V) of the car is 65 miles per hour or 110.5 km/hour or 30.7 m/sec. The kinetic energy of this car will be as follows:

$K = 1/2mv^2 = 1/2 \times 2100 \times 30.7 \times 30.7 = 1/2 \times 2100 \times 942$ (kgm^2/sec^2)

As you can see in this case, the mass of the car and its driver changes the amount of kinetic energy twice as much as the speed. It is less important if we drive on straight roads without stopping for a long distance. But usually it is in traffic or driving in the city with stopping at every light.

We are losing energy in vain.

If we analyze the situation with public transportation—buses, trains, etc.—the high speed transportation situation will be even worse than for the car. These types of transportation are heavier than the car and have many people aboard, which will wait for a few people going in and out on every stop.

It will be better to move one person on a small cart with a weight of 20 lb. that is moving by electricity directly from a grid. There is no need to have a motor in this cart—roads could provide movement automatically from your house to any destination place.

When Henry Ford produce cheap cars for millions of people he at the same time create reasons to build the roads, His cars created the road system during 20 years all around the USA.

A new transportation system could be built step by step right now.

The small weight of these carts could provide possibilities to use second and third floors of the houses and other buildings as part of these roads under roofs. Roads under roofs will save our time, money, and resources from the frustration of today's roads in snowfall conditions and other weather disasters. It will also reduce the energy for transportation by at least ten times.

We could also reduce the energy needs for moving boats by creating forces which will reduce the submerged part of the boat in its time of movement.

Power Plant

Let look at article:"Electricity generation"This page was last modified on 12 April 2012

http://en.wikipedia.org/wiki/Electricity_generation

> *"The burning of fossil fuels (coal, natural gas, or petroleum) in power plant.*
>
> *In hot gas (gas turbine) turbines are driven directly by gases produced by the combustion of natural gas or oil.*
>
> *Gas turbine plants are driven by both steam and natural gas. They generate power by burning natural gas and use residual heat to generate additional electricity from steam. These plants offer efficiencies of up to 60%.*

In a grid, we are losing more than 7% of energy. This means 11.6% of the energy of fuel.

60%-11.6%=48.4%.

According to the maximum power theorem, resistance of a source of energy must be close to the resistance of the load. In a source of energy where we are losing around 50% of energy, 48.4/2=24.2

The efficiency of the load, in average, is less than 80%. 24.2 x0.8=19.36

Not all power plants have gas turbines with up to 60% of efficiency. And if you will speak with engineers from the usual power plants, it is common to have 13% of efficiency.

As you see, the efficiency of a power plant which is common for USA is less than 20%.

When energy was cheap and nobody thought about climate change, it was okay.

It is not okay right now when not only climate change, but also dependence from foreign sources of energy dictates a new reality.

Only electrical energy could completely replace gasoline and other oil and fossil products in transportation.

Cart moving autonomously [without participation of driver] by electrical power from the grid by the roads [roads could move cart, not engine, like in today cars] will have advantages compared with today transportation. We do not need to refill the tank as it was and is in most of today's transportation system. We do not need to drive them and spend our time and attention on the road.

The more important point to understand is that it is impossible to collect GHG and heat energy from every car.

At the same time, it is not such a difficult engineering task to collect as much GHG as heat energy from one small power plant – one small plant, which is big enough to provide heat, hot water, and electricity for home and transportation use for a population of 50,000–100,000 close to this power plant.

If we change power plants to use heat as electricity, wood could provide more useful energy than coal, natural gas, or petroleum right now.

Smoke from coal, natural gas, or petroleum is toxic for forests. Smoke from wood could be put in water to water the forests surrounding power plants. Together with ash, it will be the best nutrition to grow trees.

Let's compare wood and coal by energy capacity:

1 ton coal = 16,200,000 to 26,000,000 Btu

1 ton wood = 9,000,000 to 17,000,000 Btu

In huge power plants, we are losing 80% of energy-heat energy in vain. By building small power plants all across the USA, we could provide possibilities to use wood for energy.

If we use as heat as electricity, wood will bring more useful energy than coal and oil right now.

Of course, we could also use a mix of wood, coal, natural gas, and oil products in environmentally safe proportions, especially if we solve all gases from the oven in water to watering trees. Together with ash, it will be the best nutrition to grow forests around these small power plants.

There will be close to zero emission of GHG by power plants.

Power plants with electricity, heat, and hot water could almost be only one source of energy for our needs. All gases from ovens could provide,together with ash,the best nutrition to help grow forests around power plants.

I invite readers to look carefully at next article. Scientists are trying to save the planet from carbon dioxide and other greenhouse gases and found brilliant solutions to increase the production of forests. The same solution could also be good for any vegetation.

Anthony Watts, 2011 Plant trees, not carbon laws, *ANN ARBOR, Mich.—North American forests appear to have a greater capacity to soak up heat-trapping carbon dioxide gas than researchers had previously anticipated.*

> *As a result, they could help slow the pace of human-caused climate warming more than most scientists had thought, a U-M ecologist and his colleagues have concluded."*

The reason for their research is to help slow the pace of human-caused climate change. Despite my opinion that greenhouse gases have nothing to do with climate change, their results are remarkable.

> *"The results of a 12-year study at an experimental forest in northeastern Wisconsin challenge several long-held assumptions about how future forests will respond to the rising levels of atmospheric carbon dioxide blamed for human-caused climate change, said University of Michigan microbial ecologist Donald Zak, lead author of a paper published online this week in Ecology Letters.*

"Some of the initial assumptions about ecosystem response are not correct and will have to be revised," said Zak, a professor at the U-M School of Natural Resources and Environment and the Department of Ecology and Evolutionary Biology in the College of Literature, Science, and the Arts.

To simulate atmospheric conditions expected in the latter half of this century, Zak and his colleagues continuously pumped extra carbon dioxide into the canopies of trembling aspen, paper birch and sugar maple trees at a 38-acre experimental forest in Rhinelander, Wis., from 1997 to 2008."

It is exactly what we could do with forests, surrounding power plants.

"Some of the trees were also bathed in elevated levels of ground-level ozone, the primary constituent in smog, to simulate the increasingly polluted air of the future. Both parts of the federally funded experiment—the carbon dioxide and the ozone treatments—produced unexpected results.

In addition to trapping heat, carbon dioxide is known to have a fertilizing effect on trees and other plants, making them grow faster than they normally would. Climate researchers and ecosystem modelers assume that in coming decades, carbon dioxide's fertilizing effect will temporarily boost the growth rate of northern temperate forests.

Previous studies have concluded that this growth spurt would be short-lived, grinding to a halt when the trees can no longer extract the essential nutrient nitrogen from the soil."

If previous studies are true, ammonium nitrate, which we use for food production, could be used in the forests.

"But in the Rhinelander study, the trees bathed in elevated carbon dioxide continued to grow at an accelerated rate throughout the 12-year experiment. In the final three years of the study, the CO2-soaked trees grew 26 percent more than those exposed to normal levels of carbon dioxide.

It appears that the extra carbon dioxide allowed trees to grow more small roots and "forage" more successfully for nitrogen in the soil, Zak said. At the same time, the rate at which microorganisms released nitrogen back to the soil, as fallen leaves and branches decayed, increased.

"The greater growth has been sustained by an acceleration, rather than a slowing down, of soil nitrogen cycling," Zak said. "Under elevated carbon dioxide, the trees did a better job of getting nitrogen out of the soil, and there was more of it for plants to use.

Zak stressed that growth-enhancing effects of CO2 in forests will eventually "hit the wall" and come to a halt. The trees' roots will eventually "fully exploit" the soil's nitrogen resources. No one knows how long it will take to reach that limit, he said."

As I mentioned before, even if *"the trees' roots will eventually 'fully exploit' the soil's nitrogen resources,"* we could use ammonium nitrate in the amount needed for the growth of forests.

"The ozone portion of the 12-year experiment also held surprises.

Ground-level ozone is known to damage plant tissues and interfere with photosynthesis. Conventional wisdom has held that in the future, increasing levels of ozone would constrain the degree to which rising levels of carbon dioxide would promote tree growth, canceling out some of a forest's ability to buffer projected climate warming.

In the first few years of the Rhinelander experiment, that's exactly what was observed. Trees exposed to elevated levels of ozone did not grow as fast as other trees. But by the end of study, ozone had no effect at all on forest productivity.

"What happened is that ozone-tolerant species and genotypes in our experiment more or less took up the slack left behind by those who were negatively affected, and that's called compensatory growth," Zak said. The same thing happened with growth under elevated carbon dioxide, under which some genotypes and species fared better than others."

It is very interesting research and, of course, if we decide to use wood as a source of energy, research like this will be very important directions for the nearest 20–50 years.

"The interesting take home point with this is that aspects of biological diversity— like genetic diversity and plant species compositions—are important components of an ecosystem's response to climate change," he said. "Biodiversity matters, in this regard."

The economic reasons for growing forests as sources of wood energy will provide possibilities of interesting jobs for scientists, engineers, farmers, and workers. If we change our transportation system, our heat, hot water, and electricity production, we could reduce our needs for energy at least seven times.

In 48 states, we have 600,000,000 acres of forested land. It is possible to harvest five dry tons/acre, year. The average heating value of wood is 8,000 BTU/lb(dry) or 89,596,000BTU/acre, year The consumption of energy in 2010 107,870,000,000,000,000 BTU. It is easy to calculate how big area of forest could provide this amount of energy

107,870,000,000,000,000 BTU / 89,596,000BTU/acre, year = 1,200,000,000 acres

If our energy needs for energy will be reduced seven times by changing transportation system and electricity production, we would need only 1,200,000,000/7 = 171,000,000 acres of forest.

What we are doing right now?

Let look at article by *Jeff Wilson-Mar 29,2011*

Rising Corn Acreage Seen Failing to Meet Increased U.S. Feed, Ethanol Use"

http://www.bloomberg.com/news/2011-03-29/rising-corn-acreage-seen-failing-to-meet-increased-u-s-feed-ethanol-use.html

"U.S. corn planting will expand to cover the second-largest area since World War II this year and still fail to meet demand for feed and ethanol, driving prices to their highest in at least 34 years.

Sowing will expand by 4 percent to about 91.75 million acres, the most since 2007 and the second-highest since 1944, according to a Bloomberg survey of 32 analysts. Corn will rise 5.7 percent to average $7.15 a bushel in the third quarter, the most since at least 1977, Abah Ofon and Koun-Ken Lee, analists at Standard Chartered Bank in Singapore."

As you can see, 91.75 million acres of corn will not feed the energy needs in the USA, even in transportation. In this case, we need all year to till, plant, and harvest all 91.75 million acres of land, bring harvest to ethanol producing plant, use additional energy to extract part of corn energy-ethanol Why we need all these jobs?

It is only to feed cars with real efficiency less than 1%.

In the case of forests, we need 171,000,000 acres of forest to cover all USA energy needs.

This area of forest will collect sun energy in trees during 100 years and every year we need to harvest and plant all around the USA only 1/100 of this area, or 1,710,000 acres.

In the case of corn, we must harvest during one to three weeks. In the case of forests, we could cut trees every day during the year when we need to. It means that trees will grow to feed our energy needs and evaporate water to cool the atmosphere until the last minute.

We need to burn trees both for energy and for fighting climate change.

Energy needs will provide economic reasons to grow forests. This money can save our forests better than anything else can. There are 429,000,000 acres of forests that could be a national treasure, saved by only 171,000,000 acres of forest, which we will use for our energy needs.

Only 1,710,000 acres of used forest will be cut annually. It is almost nothing if we compare that with the 91,750,000 acres of land, which every year we waste for corn with the stupid idea of ethanol production.

Even Al Gore admits that ethanol production was his mistake for political reasons.

Why do we need to use energy to take part of crop energy in the form of ethanol to feed very heavy cars, if we simply could burn trees in the form of wood to take all the energy from any sources of fuel in a power plant? We could bring electrical energy to any place and use it for the very effective transportation of small carts.

Conclusion

I hope that my main directions to fight climate change are completely understood by readers.

It is the properties of water which are actually cooling air, despite the fact that water vapor is a GHG.

All of our attempts to save the planet from global warming, and in future from global cooling, must be in the creation of evaporation on continents on level close to evaporation from oceans in every place where it is economically possible.

Following these directions, North America is a unique place on Earth. Here we have enough sources of water, despite drought in some areas. Flooding in other areas is giving us easy possibilities to relocate the water to drought areas. In this case, we could reevaluate windmills, which we use for electricity production. Dependence on the timing of wind (which does not correlate with the needs for energy) and the necessity of batteries (which reduces the efficiency of windmills by the process of charging and recharging them) make windmills the worst and most expensive source of electricity production. It will be better to use windmills as a source of energy for a pump to relocate water from flooding areas to drought areas. Almost every rain accompanies the increasing of wind. The relocation of water is crucial for flooding and drought areas, which are beneficial not only for the population there but also to evaporate water, a process which cools the atmosphere in semiarid and desert areas. Any investment in the relocation of water in the USA would bring good results for the economy, as well as for the environment. Of course, lessons from the Aral Sea must be used in any engineering project in these directions.

We can't completely restore oceans of roots, which were in North America before the Industrial Revolution. We must feed the population of USA, Canada, and Mexico. Knowing that trees have deeper roots than most other types of vegetation, we could alternate cornfields and forests. If forests provide us with the wood that could cover all our needs for energy, 91.75 million acres of cornfields for the stupid direction of ethanol production could be used for forest.

Changing our transportation system and electricity production by growing forests for wood energy and relocating water will:

1. Make North American countries energy independent.
2. Create 100% of employment in the USA, Canada, and Mexico.
3. Create possibilities to fight climate change with the help of these three countries. North America, between the Pacific, Arctic, and Atlantic oceans, influences climate from France to Japan.

The "fight with climate change" could be, and must be, very profitable.

We accelerate our lifestyles; we could accelerate processes in the parts of nature which feed us with food, energy, and other human race needs. Our needs could be achieved by directions which benefit all living species in nature, including vegetation. North America's countries are rich enough to start these directions right now and show the world a good example in the right direction.

These directions are possible, they are profitable, and they could provide jobs despite globalization.

For more than 30 years, we have been working in a globalized environment of today's level. We do not need to stop this process and return to previous situations. Let China and other development countries participate in the world economy.

We could lead the world in new directions by relocating water to semiarid areas and changing transportation from heavy cars moving by gasoline to small carts moving by electricity from the grid by roads without intersections.

Electrical power we could move efficiently for thousands miles and lose only around 7% of energy. Heat energy we could move efficiently only around 20 miles. For huge power plants it is impossible to provide customer in area 20 miles around for all created heat. That is a reason why in huge power plants we cant use heat and mostly this heat is going to nearest river, lake, ocean.

We could change our power plants from huge one using fossil fuel as its source of energy and losing 80% of its fuel energy-heat energy, to several smaller, wood burning plants—to provide electricity as heat and hot water. These plants could use wood as their main source of energy. All GHG from the plant could be solved in water to water the forests that surround these power plants. Together with ash, it could be the best nutrition to feed forests. Of course, we could also use a combination of wood, coal, oil products, and natural gas in environmentally friendly proportions in these power plants. Environmentally friendly proportions, in this case, means that we could put all gases from power plant's ovens directly into the water that waters the forest without any harm to the trees.

These great directions could provide prosperity for the USA, Canada, and Mexico. They are very simple: grow forests (we know how to do this); build small power plants, surrounding by these forests: creating new transportation system (it is very easy engineering task). It is impossible imagine any difficulties in these directions.

We could stop using fossil fuels for ground transportation, electricity, and heat. Oil, coal, and natural gas deserved to be more than our only source of energy. Chemical industries need them for many purposes, including plastic bags, which are so convenient and useful.

We have the infrastructure for cars and trains, and there is no way that we must destroy cars, trains, or our infrastructure. Everything that is economically useful we must use. At the same time, we must have the vision for good directions and escape putting money and human energy into the wrong directions.

I hope this book will change the minds of everyone who reads it carefully.

I hope that there will be a new debate in the science of climate change and new directions from dogma to science.

I hope that politicians, actors, and reporters, after reading this book, will stop agitating in the wrong directions, which have been provided by today's science of climate change. The recommendation from Kyoto, Copenhagen, and others advices from scientists of climate change for governments in the world must be our history.

I hope that every reader of this book finds something for him or herself to change the environment and prosper.

We do not need to sacrifice for the future. The future could be created together with our prosperity.

www.ingramcontent.com/pod-product-compliance
Lightning Source LLC
Chambersburg PA
CBHW070145290526
45789CB00002B/641